LEAN & GREEN
DIET COOKBOOK

The Complete Simple Guide for Beginners for Boosting Metabolism to Burn Fat and Lose Weight Fast with Lean & Green, Mouth-watering, and Energetic Diet Recipes

Sharon Rush

Legal & Disclaimer

You agree that, by continuing to read this book, where appropriate and/or necessary, you shall consult a professional (including but not limited to your doctor, attorney, financial advisor or such other advisor as needed) before using any of the suggested remedies, techniques, or information in this book.

Table of Contents

Introduction

Diets to lose weight quickly tend to be very popular. However, that does not determine their effectiveness; so, it is necessary to inquire how healthy they can be in the short and long term. In the case of the Lean & Green diet, it is said to be an excellent option not only to create a new lifestyle but to control weight with the consumption of foods rich in nutrients.

Diets that promise rapid weight loss always seem to cause a sensation, and the Lean & Green diet is no exception. But just because a diet is popular doesn't mean it really works. And in some cases, it can do you more harm than good. There are experts who claim that they can help you lose weight, but it is probably not the best option to help you lose kilos in a healthy, sustainable, and profitable way.

The Lean & Green diet is a plan for fast weight loss and is based on six meals a day intake. This includes high amounts of fiber and protein, processed or pre-packaged products and green leafy vegetables, carbohydrate restriction, and consumption of whole grains and legumes.

This diet was developed at Medifast by the developers, and although today it is very popular, it is not recommended for everyone.

When we talk about losing weight fast, we are not referring to miracle diets or restrictive diets or to doing really crazy things with our diet. We refer to diets that work in the short term that then require maintenance and that, of course, must be accompanied by consistent training to achieve our goal. For example, do you know how much weight you can lose in a week? After a "crash plan," you should continue with a balanced diet.

If you embark on a weight-loss operation, you have to be clear about one thing, only the caloric deficit works (burn more calories than consumed), either by reducing the amount of food on the plate or by frequently exercising, although the idea is to combine both options to achieve this. It will be a caloric deficit that really helps us lose fat. And, of course, choose foods with good nutritional value and not processed.

The Lean & Green diet has come to the fore as a fast and effective method to achieve this. We analyzed it to see if it is healthy.

Chapter 1.   The Lean & Green Diet

his plan is a weight loss program designed by the Medifast diet's creators, a meal replacement plan that promotes low-fat, low-calorie, and low-glycemic foods. The Lean & Green plan also encourages followers to eat six meals a day; because of this, it sells pre-packaged, portion-controlled "fuels" that are low in carbohydrates, high in protein and fiber and low in calories. Dieters are encouraged to incorporate these processed products and "lean and green" meals consisting of protein and vegetables and work with a weight loss coach.

"Fuels" include snack bars and shakes, whereas a typical "lean and green" comfort food should include 140-200 grams of protein and three servings of vegetables.

There are three diet options:

- **Plan 5 and 1:** Five Lean & Green foods and one lean green meal daily.

- **Plan 4 and 2 and 1:** Four Lean & Green foods, two lean and green meals, and one healthy snack per day.
- **Plan 3 and 3:** Three Lean & Green foods and three lean and green meals each day.

Most lean and green foods are about 300 calories or less, and fuels contain even fewer calories. So the diet cuts calories to get the desired results. The plan also encourages everyone to exercise for 30 minutes to speed up the weight loss process.

How to Follow the Lean & Green Diet

Whatever plan you choose, start a phone conversation with a coach to determine which option you intend to pursue, set weight loss goals, and become familiar with the program.

Initial Steps

1. Most people start with the Optimal Weight Plan 5 and 1 for weight loss, an 800-1,000 calorie diet that will help you lose 12 kilograms (5.4 kg) in 12 weeks.

2. In this plan, you eat 5 Lean & Green fuels and 1 Lean and Green meal daily. You should eat one meal every 2-3 hours and incorporate 30 minutes of moderate exercise most days of the week.

3. In total, Fuels and meals do not provide more than 100 grams of carbohydrates per day.

4. As Lean & Green coaches are paid for on commission, order these meals from your coach's website.

5. The purpose of Lean and Green meals is to be high in protein and low in carbohydrates. A meal offers 5-7 ounces of low-cooked protein, three servings of starch-free vegetables, and up to 2 servings of healthy fats (145-200 grams).

6. An optional daily snack is also included in this plan, which must be approved by your coach. Three sticks of celery, 1/2 cup (60 grams)

of sugar-free gelatin, or 1/2 ounce (14 grams) of nuts are the snacks approved by the plan.

7. A dining guide explaining how to order a Lean and Green meal at your favorite restaurant is also included in the program. In Plan 5 & 1, keep in mind that alcohol is strongly discouraged.

Maintenance Phase

You enter a 6-week transition phase once you reach the desired weight, which involves slowly increasing calories to no more than 1,550 calories per day and adding to a wider range of foods, including whole grains, fruits, and dairy products—low-fat content.

You need to switch to Optimal Health Plan 3 & 3 after six weeks, including 3 Lean and Green Meals and 3 Fuels per day, plus continuous training for Lean & Green.

As an Lean & Green coach, those who have sustained success in the program have the option of becoming coaches. The weight loss plan for Lean & Green 5 and 1 is low in calories and carbs and includes five pre-packaged fuels per day with one low carb and green mass. Switch to a less restrictive maintenance plan once you reach the lens's weight.

Lean & Green Diet Helps You Lose Weight

In the short term, the Lean & Green diet is effective for weight loss because the body enters a calorie deficit state given the intake of packaged products, lean proteins, and vegetables. However, it is not a long-term option, as it can cause nutritional deficiencies.

Lean & Green Diet Effectiveness

The Lean & Green diet is a weight loss diet, and in this sense, it is effective. It is a diet that can be very low in calories, below 1,200 kilocalories per day. This is about half of what a person with a standard diet and energy needs eats.

Therefore, if you strictly follow the instructions, you lose weight quickly. It is also a high protein and moderate carbohydrate plan, so you lose a good amount of fluids at first.

One of the positive points that we can comment on is that, during the diet, each person is under the supervision of a health coach, and it is recommended to perform 30 minutes of daily physical exercise. Patients are part of an active community that serves as support and counselor.

It Is Effective but Has Some Weaknesses

By putting the Lean & Green diet up for review, its weaknesses also come to light. These are the main handicaps of this plan to lose weight:

- **Rapid weight loss in a short time:** The initial rapid weight loss achieved with the Lean & Green diet can lead to dehydration and muscle mass loss. Instead, actual fat loss rarely occurs. Also, by drastically restricting the calories ingested, adverse effects such as a slowdown in basal metabolism can occur.

- **Important food restriction:** In the first phase, some large food groups are restricted. Fruits, cereals, legumes, or nuts are introduced later. This is why some nutrients may be compromised. Although all your complementary foods are fortified, the ideal would be to learn to handle all the necessary amounts and not resort to substitutes with added nutrients.

- **In the long term, it is not more effective:** In a diet ranking produced by the US News, analysts—experts in diabetes, cardiovascular health, and nutrition —concluded that maintaining the pounds lost in the long term is unlikely. Experts doubt that people will not revert to their previous eating habits. In this same analysis, of 27 types of diets—the Mediterranean, vegan, and paleo—the Lean & Green diet was below average in terms of long-term effectiveness. It obtained a score of 2.2 out of 5, always according to the experts' opinion.

- **Get little adherence:** Another major problem with the Lean & Green diet is that it is not a form of eating sustained for long. It does not achieve adherence as it is quite restrictive as it is satiating. The fact of restricting the homemade meals and the foods that can be taken in them makes it difficult to combine with family meals, social commitments, or meals in restaurants.

Some of the Disadvantages That This Diet Could Have

It Is Very Restrictive

The Lean & Green diet excludes foods (whole grains, fruits, and legumes), which contain vitamins and minerals essential for health. These restrictions affect weight loss in the long term, causing cravings and binges.

It Uses Too Many Dietary Supplements

The Lean & Green diet plans favor the intake of packaged items containing protein aggregate, and usually, they can cause stomach problems.

Besides, this diet encourages the consumption of dietary supplements not regulated by the FDA (Food and Drug Administration), so there is no guarantee of their safety or effectiveness.

It Is Not Backed by Science

To date, no research shows that the Lean & Green diet helps you healthily lose weight. The restrictions on this diet are not based on science.

It Is Very Expensive

The packaged products of the Lean & Green diet are very expensive, not to mention that you must buy lean proteins and vegetables to balance the diet and comply with the plans. That is why, in the long term, it is very difficult to maintain this regimen.

It Restricts Too Many Calories

This diet is high in protein but low in calories. About 1000 calories are consumed daily, so people who follow this regimen will experience great hunger

Lean & Green Diet and the Foods That I Can Eat

- **Meat:** Chicken, turkey, lean beef, game, lamb, pork chop or tail, ground meat (at least 85% lean)

- **Fish and shellfish:** Halibut, trout, salmon, tuna, lobster, crab, shrimp, mussels

- **Eggs:** Whole eggs, egg whites, beaten eggs

- **Soy products:** Tofu only

- **Vegetable oils:** Canola, flaxseed, walnut, and olive oil

- **Additional healthy fats:** Low-carb dressings, olives, low-Fat: margarine, almonds, nuts, pistachios, avocados

- **Low carb vegetables:** Collard greens, spinach, celery, cucumbers, mushrooms, cabbage, cauliflower, eggplant, zucchini, broccoli, peppers, spaghetti zucchini, jicama

- **Sugar-free snacks:** Popcorn, gelatin, gum, mint

- **Sugar-free drinks:** Water, unsweetened almond milk, tea, coffee

- **Spices and seasonings:** Dried herbs, spices, salt, lemon juice, lemon juice, yellow mustard, soy sauce, salsa, sugar-free syrup, calorie-free sweeteners, 1/2 teaspoon only ketchup, cocktail sauce, or grilled sauce

Recommended Foods to Avoid

- **Fried food:** Meat, fish, shellfish, vegetables, sweets such as pastries

- **Refined cereals:** White bread, pasta, biscuits, pancakes, flour tortillas, biscuits, white rice, cakes, cakes, pastries

- **Certain fats:** Butter, coconut oil, solid shortening

- **Whole fat dairy products:** Milk, cheese, yogurt

- **Alcohol:** All varieties

- **Sugar-sweetened beverages:** Soda, fruit juice, sports drinks, energy drinks, sweet tea

The following foods are outside the limits on plan 5 & 1 but are added back in the 6-week transition phase and are allowed during plan 3 & 3:

- **Fruits:** All fresh fruits

- **Low-Fat: or Fat-free dairy products:** Yogurt, milk, cheese

- **Whole grains:** Wholemeal bread, rich breakfast cereals, brown rice, wholemeal pasta

- **Legumes:** Peas, lentils, beans, soy

- **Starchy vegetables:** Sweet potatoes, white potatoes, corn, peas

In the transition phase and Plan 3 and 3, you are especially encouraged to eat berries over other fruits, as they are lower in carbohydrates.

Lean & Green Diet Costs

Regardless of which plan you choose, you should know that this diet is not cheap. According to the website, kits range from $ 350–450 per month (about € 285–366). And you will also have to buy additional food to prepare the healthy meals that you cook on your own at home.

People Who Should Not Follow the Lean & Green Diet

- People who have a condition such as diabetes, irritable bowel syndrome, or celiac disease. These types of illnesses require choosing the foods to consume, and, due to the restrictions of this regimen, it will not be possible.

- It is not recommended for pregnant women or those who have just had a child. The reason is that this diet only consumes 1000 to 1100 calories, which is very little for a person who is in condition or breastfeeding.

- If you take certain medications, as some ingredients in these supplements are not regulated, they can have unfavorable interactions with certain medications.

The recommendation is to consult a doctor before starting this or any diet plan. You need to make sure that it is safe for health and sustainable in the long term.

Lean & Green Programs

The general rules are simple since almost everything is already prepackaged. Here they are:

- Consume food approximately every 3 hours;

- Drink not less than 2 liters of water per day;

- Strictly respect the Lean & Green meals;

- The allowed proteins must not exceed a total of 200g per day;

- Daily cardio training is also mandatory;

- Sleep 8 hours a night;

- Based on the pounds to lose, meal plans can be chosen.

Program 5 & 1

The most rigid choice (and crazy, I add, but crazy) is the 5 + 1: 800-1000 kcal, 5 Lean & Green meals per day + 1 meal of vegetables and proteins.

Program 4 & 2

The official website is an intermediate, transitional option: it provides a gradual increase in caloric intake. In this case, 4 Lean & Green meals per day + 2 meals of vegetables and proteins + 1 Lean & Green snack.

Maintenance Program

It is called 3 & 3 and should be followed for six weeks. It consists of taking 3 Lean & Green meals per day + 3 meals of vegetables and proteins.

Lean & Green Exercise Program Even if You Have No Time

- **Aerobic exercise:** Among other things, walking, running, and cycling burns calories help strengthen your lungs and heart. Aim for at least three days of moderate aerobic exercises per week. You do not have to do all 30 minutes at once; you can exercise up to 30 minutes a day in 10-minute sessions. Examples of light-to-moderate exercise include gardening, walking, tai chi, yoga, tennis, dancing, and hiking.

- **Strength training:** It includes weight/load lifting or pushing. The idea is to increase the weight as you get stronger. Muscles adapt quickly and develop best when constantly challenged. You should train all your major muscle groups 2-3 times a week.

- **Lifestyle exercise:** This allows you to increase your activity level through daily activities such as shopping, cleaning, going to work, or caring for your home and yard. Set a 30-45-minute lifestyle exercise goal each weekday.

How the Diet Transforms Your State of Mind

When people go on a diet, they often are not in the right mindset. You have to make a decision on why you are going on a diet and why it is important to you.

If you just want to lose weight, you should say it with conviction and determination to make it last a little longer so you can look good in a bathing suit for the summer.

The plan is much clearer and more specific. If you go on a diet and restrict yourself too much, you are likely to binge and give up your progress.

You need to realize the importance of your mindset when pursuing your weight loss goals. Do not look at a diet as a crash diet to drop a bunch of weight fast. It is a lifestyle change. Including increased physical activity, whether it is weight training, jogging, or playing with your kids in the park. It can add up to lots of calories, so physical activity is a good way to lose weight. As you get used to it, you will have more energy to do fun things.

A second piece of the lifestyle change is diet. The best way to lose weight is to omit bad foods and opt for healthy ones. These are processed foods, foods with white flour and sugars. You should eat fresh foods. Foods contain all sorts of different substances.

Focus on changing your attitude and lifestyle to lose weight. It is something that you can stick to and lead you to change your lifestyle. Learn about good exercise and eating habits, and you will feel better and lose weight.

What Lean & Green Health Coach Can Do

- Provide guidance and encouragement to clients for lifelong transformation related to LEAN & GREEN program meal plans, product choices, exercise, and general direction.

- Provide clients with one-on-one support as it relates to the health system's habits.

- Engage and promote the participation of clients in the LEAN & GREEN Community, including support activities (i.e., calls, webinars, events, etc.).

- Inform Nutrition Support of program and/or adverse product reactions (e.g., if a Client is hospitalized etc.).

Chapter 2. Lean & Green Fueling Recipes

Biscuit Based Cheesecake

Preparation: 40 min, ready in 1 h. 20 min.

Nutritional values:

- Calories: 418 kcal (20%)

- Protein: 16g (16%)

- Fat: 27g (23%)

- Carbohydrates: 28g (19%)

- Added sugar: 17g (68%)

- Fiber: 4.4g (15%)

Ingredients:

- 150g Whole grain biscuit
- 50g Butter
- 1 Tbsp. Beet syrup
- 500g Ricotta
- 300g Low-Fat quark
- 2 Eggs
- 2 Tbsp. cornstarch
- ½ Tsp. vanilla powder
- 50g Raw cane sugar
- 100g Chopped almond
- 150g Small candy bars
- 150ml Whipped cream

Preparation steps:

1. Place the biscuits in a clean tea towel and use the pin to crush them into crumbs. Melt butter over low heat in a small saucepan and mix with crumbs and beet syrup. Line the baker's springform pan. Pour the biscuit mixture and press firmly.

2. Combine ricotta and quark. Gradually add eggs, cornstarch whisk, vanilla, and sugar. Fold the cream and almonds. Place the bars on the cake base and smooth the cream over them. Bake 50–60 minutes in a preheated oven (convection 160°C; gas: level 2–3).

3. Take the cheesecake off the oven and let it cool in the pan. Remove the cheesecake and let it cool down completely.

4. Whip the cream until stiff and serve with cake.

5.

Yogurt Quark Layered Dish

Preparation: 10 min.

Nutritional values:

- Calories: 311 kcal (15%)

- Protein: 12g (12%)

- Fat: 7g (6%)

- Carbohydrates: 48g (32%)

- Added sugar: 13g (52%)

- Fiber: 3.5g (12%)

Ingredients:

- 40g Ladyfingers (6 ladyfingers)

- 2 Tbsp. Passion fruit juice

- 75g Strawberries (6 strawberries)

- 2 Tbsp. yogurt (1.5% Fat:)

- 1 Tbsp. Low-fat quark

- 2 Half apricots (can)

- 1 Tsp. Pistachios

- 1 Tsp. Honey

Preparation steps:

1. Spread the ladyfingers in a small flat bowl and drizzle evenly with the passion fruit juice.

2. Clean and wash the strawberries and put one nice berry aside. Cut the rest of the berries into small cubes and sprinkle them over the ladyfingers.

3. Stir yogurt and quark in a small bowl until creamy. Distribute strawberries evenly.

4. Drain the apricot halves into narrow wedges.

5. Chop pistachios roughly.

6. Place the strawberry in the middle of the layered dish, and arrange the apricot wedges around it like flower petals. Sprinkle with pistachios, honey, and serve.

Chocolate Bar With Caramel

Preparation: 50 min, ready in 5 h. 40 min.

Nutritional value

- calories: 285kcal,
- carbohydrates: 39g,
- Protein: 3g,
- Fat: 13g,

Ingredients:

For the dough:

- 300g Flour and some divided flour to work with
- 100g Sugar
- 1 Pinch salt
- 200g Butter
- 1 Egg

- Dried pulses for blind baking

For the caramel layer:

- 600ml Whipped cream
- 300g Sugar
- 75g Butter
- 75ml Whiskey cream liqueur
- 400g Dark chocolate coverture

For the chocolate layer:

- 400g Dark chocolate coverture

Preparation steps:

1. Put the flour on the work surface and form a hollow in the middle. Spread the sugar, salt, and butter on the flour edge. Put the egg in the middle and chop the crumbs with a pastry card. Knead with your hands to form a smooth dough no longer sticking to your hands. Wrap in film and put in the fridge for about 30 minutes.

2. Preheat fan oven to 180°C. Line a deep parchment-paper baking sheet.

3. Roll out the dough to a sheet size on a floured surface and place it on the baking sheet. With a fork, pinch the bottom several times, cover with baking paper and legumes. Bake for 15-20 minutes until golden. Remove the legumes and paper and let it cool on the baking sheet.

4. Cook cream, sugar, butter, and liqueur in a saucepan for the caramel layer while stirring over low heat for about 30 minutes, occasionally stirring (up to about 1/3) until golden yellow and thick. Remove from heat, stir in chopped chocolate, and let it cool down.

5. Put the mixture on the floor and smooth. Let it cool down for about 2 hours.

6. Chop the cover to coat, melt over a hot water bath and let it cool down. Smooth on the caramel layer, set for about 1 hour.

7. Serve in pieces.

Chocolate Nut Bars

Preparation: 30 min, ready in 52 min.

Nutritional values:

- Calories: 283 kcal (13%)

- Protein: 6g (6%)

- Fat: 20g (17%)

- Carbohydrates: 21g (14%)

- Added sugar: 19g (76%)

- Fiber: 4.3g (14%)

Ingredients:

1. 175g Biscuit z. b. whole grain or shortbread biscuits

2. 200g Roasted almond kernels

3. 75g Brown sugar

4. 150g Melted butter

5. 400g Coconut flakes

6. 350g Sweetened condensed milk

7. 500g Dark chocolate coverture

Preparation steps:

1. Preheat the oven to 175°C lower and upper heat.

2. For the base, crumble the biscuits coarsely and finely crumble them with 75g almonds and the sugar in a lightning chopper. Mix in the butter and press evenly flat in a baking pan lined with baking paper (approx. 32x24 cm)—Bake in the oven for about 20 minutes.

3. Mix the coconut flakes with the condensed milk. Take the bottom out of the oven and spread the coconut mixture on top. Sprinkle with the remaining almonds and bake in the oven for another 10 minutes. Then take it out of the oven again.

4. Chop the chocolate and let it melt over a hot water bath. Let it cool down a little, spread it on the cake, and let it cool down on a wire rack (in the fridge if necessary).

5. Cut into pieces before serving.

Cream Slices With Raspberries

Preparation: 2 h. 40 min.

Nutritional values:

- Calories: 354 kcal (17%)

- Protein: 30g (31%)

- Fat: 19g (16%)

- Carbohydrates: 14g (9%)

- Added sugar: 1g (4%)

- Fiber: 4.5g (15%)

Ingredients:

- 250g Raspberries

- 2 Sheets gelatin

- 2 Tbsp. Raspberry liqueur

- 150g Mascarpone

- 200g Whipped cream

- 3 Tbsp. Cane sugar

- 1 Packet vanilla sugar

- 1 Packet cream stiffener

- 6 Nut and granola bars

- Lemon balm for garnish

Preparation steps:

1. Wash and sort the berries. Puree approx. 1/4 of it and strain through a sieve. Soak the gelatin in cold water. Then squeeze out and dissolve in the warm liqueur. Stir into the puree.

2. Mix the mascarpone until smooth with the sugar and vanilla sugar, whip the cream until stiff with the cream stiffener and fold in the mascarpone, then stir in the raspberry puree.

3. Put together the muesli bars with their long sides and frame them with aluminum foil (approx. 5 cm high). On the muesli platter, spread 3/4 of the cream, pour the raspberry puree on top and spread the rest of the cream on top. Min. Min. Just chill for two hours. Cut into six slices with a hot knife (dip in hot water briefly) and garnish with the remaining berries and lemon balm to serve.

Healthy Hot Chocolate

Preparation: 10 min

Nutritional values:

- Calories: 150 kcal (7%)

- Protein: 11g (11%)

- Fat: 3g (3%)

- Carbohydrates: 18g (12%)

- Added sugar: 0g (0%)

- Fiber: 6.6g (22%)

Ingredients:

- 1 ½ Tsp. Cocoa powder

- 1 Pinch cinnamon

- 2 Pitted soft dates

- 250ml Almond drink (almond milk) or another plant-based milk alternative

- Cocoa nibs or vegan spray cream as desired

Preparation steps:

1. Crush the cocoa with cinnamon, soft dates (2 or 3 depending on the desired sweetness), and plant-based milk of your choice with a hand blender until the dates are finely pureed.

2. Slowly heat the mixture in a saucepan.

3. Pour into a cup and top the hot chocolate with (vegan) spray cream, cocoa nibs, and some cocoa powder if you like.

Spicy Hot Chocolate

Preparation: 10 min, ready in 15 min

Nutritional values:

- Calories: 239 kcal (11%)

- Protein: 10g (10%)

- Fat: 12g (10%)

- Carbohydrates: 22g (15%)

- Added sugar: 4g (16%)
- Fiber: 6g (20%)

Ingredients:

- 5g Chili pepper
- 30g Ginger in one piece
- 1 Vanilla pod
- 70g Dark chocolate (at least 70% cocoa content, vegan)
- 400ml Almond drink (almond milk)
- 2 Cinnamon sticks
- 3-star anise
- Cinnamon powder

Preparation steps:

1. Wash the chili pepper and ginger and cut into small pieces. Halve the vanilla pod, scrape out the pulp, and set it aside. Roughly chop the chocolate and also set it aside.

2. Put the almond drink with chili, ginger, scraped vanilla pod, cinnamon sticks, and star anise in a saucepan and heat. Cover and let simmer over low heat for about 10 minutes.

3. Pour the spiced drink through a sieve into a bowl and reheat the liquid in the pot. Stir in vanilla pulp and chopped chocolate and let melt.

4. Divide the Spicy Hot Chocolate between two mugs, sprinkle with cinnamon and enjoy hot.

Mashed Potatoes

Preparation: 30 min, ready in 1 h.

Nutritional values:

- Calories: 253 kcal (12%)

- Protein: 5.6g (6%)

- Fat: 10.1g (9%)

- Carbohydrates: 33.6g (22%)

- Added sugar: 0g (0%)

- Fiber: 2.5g (8%)

Ingredients:

- 800g Floury potatoes

- Salt

- 200ml Lukewarm milk (3.5% Fat:)

- 40g Butter in flakes

- Pepper from the mill

- Freshly grated nutmeg

Preparation steps:

1. Peel and wash the potatoes and cook in salted boiling water for about 30 minutes. Drain, allow to evaporate and press through a potato press.

2. Mix with the milk and butter to a smooth puree. Serve the mashed potatoes seasoned with salt, pepper, and nutmeg.

Pollack With Coconut Crust and Thai Vegetables

Preparation: 45 min.

Nutritional values:

- Calories: 773 kcal (37%)

- Protein: 39g (40%)

- Fat: 45g (39%)

- Carbohydrates: 52g (35%)

- Added sugar: 0g (0%)

- Fiber 10g (33%)

Ingredients:

- 600g Pollack fillet
- Salt
- Pepper
- 6 Tbsp. Lime juice
- 600g Small sweet potatoes (2 small sweet potatoes)
- 2 Tbsp. Liquid coconut oil
- Chili Powder
- 300g Green beans
- 5 Spring onions
- 4 Stems Thai basil
- 75g Peanut butter (5 Tbsp.)
- 30g Desiccated coconut (4 Tbsp.)
- 1 Shallot
- 10g Ginger
- 1 Tsp. Sesame oil
- 400ml of coconut milk

Preparation steps:

1. Rinse the pollack fillet, pat dry, cut into four pieces, season with salt and pepper, drizzle with two tablespoons of lime juice, and let it be steep for 10 minutes.

2. In the meantime, peel the sweet potatoes for the vegetables, cut in half lengthways, and cut into slices. Heat 1 tablespoon of coconut oil

in a large pan and fry sweet potato slices over medium heat for 6–7 minutes. Then season with salt, pepper, and chili powder.

3. Simultaneously, clean and wash the beans and cook in salted boiling water for 10 minutes on low heat; then quench and drain. Clean and wash the spring onions and cut diagonally into fine rings. Wash the Thai basil, shake dry and remove the leaves.

4. Pat the fish pieces dry on one side, brush thinly with 1 Tbsp. Peanut butter each and press this side into the desiccated coconut, place in a baking dish, drizzle with the remaining coconut oil and bake in a preheated oven at 200 ° C (convection 180 ° C; gas: level 3). Bake until golden brown in 15–20 minutes.

5. Meanwhile, peel and chop the shallot and ginger for the sauce. Heat the sesame oil in a pan, fry shallot, and ginger for 2 minutes over medium heat. Stir in the rest of the peanut butter, pour in coconut milk, and simmer over low heat for 10 minutes. Season the sauce with the rest of the lime juice, salt, and chili to taste.

6. Arrange the beans and sweet potatoes in a wide bowl and drizzle with the sauce. Place the fish crust up on the vegetables and sprinkle with basil leaves and spring onions.

Coconut Cream Cake With Chocolate Base

Preparation: 45 min. Ready in 2 h. 10 min.

Nutritional values:

- Calories: 389 kcal (19%)

- Protein: 7g (7%)

- Fat: 26g (22%)

- Carbohydrates: 33g (22%)

- Added sugar: 9g (36%)

- Fiber: 2.9g (10%)

Ingredients:

- 2 Eggs

- 1 Pinch salt

- 80g Agave syrup

- 125g Butter

- 220g Wheat flour type 1050 or spelled flour 1050

- ½ Packet baking powder

- 30g Cocoa powder (heavily de-oiled)

- 1 Packet vanilla pudding powder

- 400ml Coconut milk (9% Fat)

- 30g Coconut blossom sugar

- 40g Coconut flakes

- 4 Sheets gelatin

- 150ml Whipped cream

- 100g Dark chocolate

- 20g Coconut oil

Preparation steps:

1. Separate the eggs and beat the egg whites with salt to form egg whites. Mix agave syrup with butter and egg yolk until frothy. Mix the flour, baking powder, and cocoa and sift into the egg yolk foam, then work into a smooth dough and very carefully fold in the egg whites.

2. Line the springform pan with baking paper or grease. Pour in the dough, smooth it out and bake at 180°C (convection 160°C; gas: level 2) for about 25-30 minutes (make a stick test). Then let the cake cool in the pan.

3. In the meantime, stir the pudding powder with 5–6 tablespoons of coconut milk until smooth. Put the remaining coconut milk, coconut blossom sugar, and 30g coconut flakes in a saucepan and bring to the boil. Stir in the mixed pudding powder, bring to the boil while stirring, and then allow to cool.

4. Soak the gelatine in cold water. Whip 100ml cream until stiff. Slightly heat the rest of the cream in a saucepan and dissolve the well-squeezed gelatine in it. Stir in 4 tablespoons of the coconut cream and then add to the rest of the coconut cream. Fold in the cream and smooth the cream on the chocolate base. Chill for at least 1 hour.

5. Roughly, chop the dark chocolate and melt it with the coconut oil over a water bath, allow to cool a little. In the meantime, carefully, remove the cake from the mold. Cover the cake with chocolate icing. Sprinkle with the remaining coconut flakes and allow to set. Serve cut into pieces.

Poppyseed Cheesecake With Coconut

Preparation: 45 min. Ready in 1 h. 35 min.

Nutritional values:

- Calories: 528 kcal (25%)

- Protein: 17g (17%)

- Fat: 29g (25%)

- Carbohydrates: 49g (33%)

- Added sugar: 16.6g (66%)

- Fiber: 5.5g (18%)

Ingredients:

- 100ml Apple juice

- 80g Dried apricots

- 1 Organic lemon

- 200g Butter

- 300g Coconut blossom sugar

- 8 Eggs

- 450g Wheat flour type 1050

- 2 Tbsp. cocoa powder (heavily de-oiled)

- 2 Tsp. baking powder

- 150ml milk (3.5% Fat)

- 150g Poppyseed baking

- 500g Marzipan paste

- 500g Low-Fat quark

- 500g Cream cheese

- 1 Tbsp. Lemon juice

- 1 Packet vanilla pudding powder

- 1 Pinch salt

- 120g Coconut flakes

Preparation steps:

1. Soak apricots in apple juice. Wash lemon with hot water, rub dry, rub peel and squeeze out the juice.

2. For the batter, stir the butter with 150g coconut blossom sugar and one teaspoon lemon zest until creamy and gradually stir in 4 eggs. Mix flour with cocoa and baking powder and fold alternately with milk into the butter and egg mixture. Drain the apricots, chop them up and mix them into the batter with the poppy seeds.

3. Spread half of the batter on a baking sheet lined with baking paper and prebake in a preheated oven at 180 ° C (convection 160 ° C; gas: level 2-3) for about 10 minutes.

4. Take out and let it cool down.

5. Roll out the marzipan between 2 layers of cling film and cut into wide strips. Lay these on the dough base.

6. Separate the remaining eggs and mix the egg yolks with the quark, cream cheese, remaining coconut blossom sugar, one tablespoon lemon juice, and vanilla pudding powder. Beat the egg white with a pinch of salt until stiff and fold into the cheese mixture. Spread the mixture on the marzipan, spread the remaining sponge mixture on it, a tablespoon at a time, bake the cake in the hot oven in about 40 minutes, and make a stick test.

7. Take the finished cake out of the oven, let it cool down, and sprinkle with coconut flakes.

Chocolate Pudding With Caramel

Preparation: 30 min. Ready in 1 hour

Nutritional values:

- Calories: 521 kcal (25%)

- Protein: 8g (8%)

- Fat: 35g (30%)

- Carbohydrates: 45g (30%)

- Added sugar: 41g (164%)

- Fiber: 1.8g (6%)

Ingredients:

For the cream:

- 50g Sugar

- 1 Egg

- 2 Egg yolks

- 75g Dark chocolate

- 200ml of milk

- 150ml Whipped cream at least 30% Fat: content

- Oil for the molds

Preparation steps:

1. Beat the sugar with the egg and egg yolks. Roughly chop the chocolate, bring to the boil with the milk and cream in a saucepan and let it flow into the egg mixture while stirring. For the caramel mirror, simmer the sugar with two tablespoons of water in a small saucepan until the sugar is golden brown. Immediately pour into the lightly oiled molds and toss until the caramel is evenly distributed on the molds' bottom.

2. Preheat the oven to an upper and lower heat of 200 ° C. Pour the egg-milk through a sieve and fill the molds. Place the molds in a

baking dish and fill half of the molds with boiling water. Let it set in the preheated oven for about 30 minutes. Let the cream cool and turn it out onto a plate to serve.

Lentil and Potato Soup

Preparation: 25 min.

Nutritional values:

- Calories: 351 kcal (17%)

- Protein: 12g (12%)

- Fat: 16g (14%)

- Carbohydrates: 40g (27%)

- Added sugar: 0g (0%)

- Fiber: 8.7g (29%)

Ingredients:

- 3 Carrots

- 250g Potatoes

- 2 Tbsp. Olive oil

- 100g Red lentils

- ½ Tsp. Turmeric powder

- 1 l Vegetable broth

- 120g Tomato paste (8 Tbsp.)

- Salt

- Pepper

- 120g Whipped cream

- 2 Discs sourdough wholemeal bread (50g each)

- 5g basil (1 handful)

Preparation steps:

1. Clean, peel and cut the carrots and potatoes into small cubes. Heat 1 tablespoon of oil in a saucepan. Sauté the carrots and potatoes in it over medium heat for 4 minutes. Add lentils and turmeric and cook for 2 minutes.

2. Add the vegetable broth and tomato paste and season with salt and pepper. Let the soup simmer over low heat for about 15 minutes. Add 100g cream and puree with a hand blender.

3. At the same time, dice bread slices. Heat the remaining oil in a pan. Roast the bread cubes in it for 5 minutes over medium heat until golden brown. Wash the basil, shake dry and pick off the leaves. Pour the soup into bowls, drizzle with the remaining cream and sprinkle with bread cubes and basil.

Vegetable and Lentil Stew With Peas

Preparation: 25 min.

Nutritional values:

- Calories: 592 kcal (28%)

- Protein: 21g (21%)

- Fat: 23g (20%)

- Carbohydrates: 74g (49%)

- Added sugar: 0g (0%)

- Fiber: 16.7g (56%)

Ingredients:

- 5g Ginger tuber

- 1 Shallot

- 1 Sweet potato

- 100g Celery root

- 2 Tbsp. Olive oil

- 80g Red lentils

- 1 Tsp. Harissa paste

- 1 Tbsp. Tomato paste

- ½ Tsp. Curry powder

- 600ml Vegetable broth

- Salt

- Pepper

- 4 Tbsp. Coconut milk

- 2 Pieces spring onions

- 150g Frozen pea

- 2 Tsp. Sunflower seeds

Preparation steps:

1. Peel and chop the ginger and shallot. Clean and peel the sweet potato and celery and cut into small cubes.

2. Heat 1 tablespoon of oil in a saucepan, sauté the ginger, shallot, sweet potato, and celery over medium heat for 5 minutes. Add lentils, harissa, tomato paste, curry powder, and sauté for 4 minutes.

3. Pour the vegetable stock, season with salt and pepper, and let the soup simmer for about 15 minutes. Then stir in 2 tablespoons of coconut milk.

4. At the same time, clean, wash and chop the spring onions. Heat the remaining oil in a pan, fry the onion, peas, and sunflower seeds for 5 minutes. Fill the soup into two bowls, drizzle with the remaining coconut milk, and top with the peas.

Braised Beef in Red Wine Sauce

Preparation: 50 min. Ready in 3 h. 20 min.

Nutritional values:

- Calories: 558 kcal (27%)

- Protein: 46g (47%)

- Fat: 25g (22%)

- Carbohydrates: 22g (15%)

- Added sugar: 0g (0%)

- Fiber: 5g (17%)

Ingredients:

- 800g Beef ready to cook, off the shoulder

- 4 Tbsp. rapeseed oil

- Salt

- Pepper

- Paprika noble sweet

- 6 Onions

- 1 Tbsp. Tomato paste

- 400ml of dry red wine z. b. burgundy

- 200ml of beef stock

- 300g Young, small Festkochend potatoes

- 1 Carrot

- ½ Rod leek

- 200g Mushrooms

- 2 Bay leaves

- 3 Peppercorns

- 1 Piece lemon peel

- 2 Tbsp. Coarsely chopped parsley

Preparation steps:

1. Wash the meat, pat dry, and cut into bite-sized pieces.

2. Fry the meat in 2 Tbsp. rapeseed oil in portions and season with salt, pepper, and paprika, then remove. Peel and finely chop the onions and sauté in the remaining oil. Stir in the tomato paste, let it take color briefly, then put the meat back in and pour in the wine and the stock. Let it simmer over low heat for about 1 1/2 hours.

3. In the meantime, wash and clean the vegetables. Halve the potatoes, peel the carrot and cut into sticks. Quarter the leek lengthways and cut into 3 cm long pieces. Clean and chop the mushrooms.

4. Fry the vegetables and mushrooms briefly in 2 tablespoons of rapeseed oil, add to the meat with the spices at the end of the cooking time and simmer for 45 minutes on low heat.

5. Remove the spices again, season the stew with salt and pepper and serve sprinkled with freshly chopped parsley. Serve with a fresh baguette if you like.

Chapter 3.   Lean and Green Combines Salads

Bean and Mozzarella Salad

Preparation: 20 min.

Nutritional values:

- Calories: 98 kcal (5%)

- Protein: 7g (7%)

- Fat: 5g (4%)

- Carbohydrates: 5g (3%)

- Added sugar: 0g (0%)

- Fiber: 3.5g (12%)

Ingredients:

- 100g Green beans

- Salt

- 10g Ginger (1 piece)

- 2 Stems flat-leaf parsley

- 4 Stems coriander

- ½ Lime

- 50ml Mediterranean vegetable broth

- Pepper

- 50g Mozzarella (9% Fat)

Preparation steps:

1. Wash the beans, drain them, clean them and cook for about 10 minutes in salted boiling water.

2. Meanwhile, peel the ginger and finely grate it. Wash the coriander and the parsley, shake it dry, and pull the leaves off.

3. Squeeze the lime and pour the juice into a tall container with the leaves of ginger, parsley, and coriander.

4. Use a hand blender to purée everything, and pour in the broth. Season the salt and pepper with pesto.

5. Drain the mozzarella and dice it out.

6. Drain, and arrange the beans with the mozzarella on plates. Spread on the top of the pesto and serve.

Baked May Beets With a Sesame Crust

Preparation: 30 min. Ready in 45 min

Nutritional values:

- Calories: 166 kcal (8%)

- Protein: 7g (7%)

- Fat: 9g (8%)

- Carbohydrates: 12g (8%)

- Added sugar: 0g (0%)

- Fiber: 9g (30%)

Ingredients:

- 1kg Small beets (6 small beets)

- 1½ Tbsp. Germ oil

- Salt

- 1 Chive (small bunch)

- 2 Eggs

- 40g Unpeeled sesame seeds

- 2 Tbsp. Wholegrain breadcrumbs

- 150g Baby salad mix

- 2 Tbsp. White balsamic vinegar

- Pepper

Preparation steps:

1. Clean, peel and halve the beets.

2. Brush the bottom of a flat baking dish with 1/2 Tbsp. oil. Put in the beets with the cut surfaces facing up. If necessary, cut a little flatter on the underside not to tip over.

3. Sprinkle the beets with salt. Close the tin with aluminum foil and cook the beets in the preheated oven on the middle rack at 200 ° C (convection 180 ° C, gas level 3) for about 20 minutes.

4. In the meantime, wash the chives, shake dry and cut into fine rolls.

5. Separate eggs. Beat egg white with a pinch of salt until stiff. Fold in the sesame seeds, chives, and breadcrumbs. Use egg yolks elsewhere.

6. Spread the mixture over the pre-baked beets. Return the beets to the oven and bake for another 10-15 minutes at the same temperature.

7. In the meantime, clean the lettuce, wash and spin dry, mix vinegar, salt, pepper, and remaining oil to a vinaigrette.

8. Mix the salad with the vinaigrette and divide it over four plates. Arrange the baked beets on top.

Vegetable Sticks With Quark and Caviar Dip

Preparation: 20 min

Nutritional values:

- Calories: 137 kcal (7%)

- Protein: 13g (13%)

- Fat: 4g (3%)

- Carbohydrates: 11g (7%)

- Added sugar: 0g (0%)

- Fiber 4.5g (15%)

Ingredients:

- 150g Green zucchini (1 green zucchini)

- 150g Yellow zucchini (1 yellow zucchini)

- 200g Red pepper (1 red pepper)

- 150g Carrots (1 carrot)

- 100g Cucumber (0.5 cucumbers)

- 80g Celery (1 stick)

- 1 Chive

- 1 Organic lemon

- 150g Low-Fat quark

- 125g Yogurt alternative made from natural soy

- 150g Caviar (e.g., trout, algae, or salmon caviar)

- Salt

- Pepper

Preparation steps:

1. Wash and clean the vegetables, peel them if necessary, and cut them into bite-sized pieces.

2. Wash the chives, shake dry and cut into fine rolls.

3. Rinse the lemon with hot water, rub dry and finely grate the peel.

4. Squeeze the lemon.

5. Mix the quark and soy yogurt alternative with chives, lemon zest, and a little lemon juice in a bowl.

6. Fold in caviar and season with salt and pepper. Serve with the prepared vegetable sticks.

Chicken Pot With Pears and Beans

Preparation: 20 minutes ready in 30 minutes

Nutritional values:

- Calories: 381 kcal (18%)

- Protein: 41g (42%)

- Fat: 16g (14%)

- Carbohydrates: 17g (11%)

- Added sugar: 0g (0%)

- Fiber: 7g (23%)

Ingredients:

- 300g Chicken breast fillet (2 chicken breast fillets)

- Salt

- Pepper

- 1 Onion

- 2 Cooking pears

- ½ Lemon

- 1 Tbsp. Oil (e.g., sunflower oil)

- 2 Juniper berries

- 1 Bay leaf

- 200g Green beans (fresh or frozen)

- 150ml Classic vegetable broth

- ½ Fret parsley

- 30g Walnut kernels (2 Tbsp.)

Preparation steps:

1. Rinse the chicken breast fillets, pat dry with kitchen paper, and cut into 2 x 2 cm cubes—season with salt and pepper.

2. Peel the onion and chop finely.

3. Wash the pears, rub dry, cut in half, and eighth. Cut out the core casing. Squeeze the lemon half.

4. Heat the oil in a saucepan and sauté the onion cubes. Add the chicken cubes and stir-fry for 1–2 minutes. Also, add the juniper and bay leaf and fry for another 1–2 minutes.

5. Add the peas and beans (first wash the fresh beans and cut off the tips) and sauté for 1 minute, stirring constantly.

6. Pour in the lemon juice and vegetable stock and cook everything over medium heat for about 15 minutes.

7. In the meantime, wash the parsley, shake dry, pluck the leaves off and chop.

8. Also, chop walnuts with a large knife. Sprinkle with the parsley over the chicken pot and serve.

Grilled Green Asparagus

Preparation: 40 min.

Nutritional values:

- Calories: 205 kcal (10%)

- Protein: 7g (7%)

- Fat: 14g (12%)

- Carbohydrates: 11g (7%)

- Added sugar: 0g (0%)

- Fiber: 6.5g (22%)

Ingredients:

- 2 Red onions

- 45g Pistachios (3 Tbsp.)

- 1 Orange

- 1 Lime

- 2 Tomatoes

- Salt

- Pepper

- 3 Tbsp. Olive oil

- 4 Stems basil

- 20 Bars green asparagus

- 1 Tbsp. Balsamic vinegar

Preparation steps:

1. Peel the onions and finely dice them.

2. Hang a colander in a pot of boiling water. Scatter onion cubes and cook for 30 seconds. Lift the sieve out of the water, rinse the onion cubes in cold water and drain well.

3. Finely chop the pistachios. Peel the orange with a knife thick enough to remove the white skin.

4. Cut the orange into slices and roughly chop. Squeeze the lime.

5. Wash, quarter and core the tomatoes, removing the stalks. Finely dice the tomato flesh.

6. Mix with onion cubes, orange pieces, 1 Tbsp. lime juice, salt, pepper, and 2 Tbsp. olive oil.

7. Wash the basil, shake dry and roughly chop the leaves. Mix in the basil and pistachios. Set the salsa aside.

8. Wash the asparagus. Cut off the lower woody end of the asparagus stalks. If desired, peel the stalks in the lower third.

9. Place five stalks of asparagus next to each other on the work surface and fix in 2 places with wooden skewers; this makes turning easier and ensures an even tan.

10. Heat the grilling pan and brush the remaining olive oil with the asparagus spears.

11. For 3-4 minutes on each side, grill in the pan until al dente. Season with salt and pepper and serve with the salsa. Deglaze with vinegar.

Boiled Beef Stew With Green Beans

Preparation: 1 h. 40 min.

Nutritional values:

- Calories: 317 kcal (15%)

- Protein: 43g (44%)

- Fat: 8g (7%)

- Carbohydrates: 14g (9%)

- Added sugar: 0g (0%)

- Fiber: 5.5g (18%)

Ingredients:

- 3 Onions

- 800g Boiled beef

- Salt

- Pepper

- 2 Tbsp. Rapeseed oil

- 1200ml of Beef broth

- 600g Green beans

- 500g Potatoes

- 3 Stems of savory

- 3 Stems of parsley

- 50g Fresh horseradish (1 piece)

Preparation steps:

1. Peel the onions and cut them into fine strips.

2. Cut the boiled beef into 3 cm cubes and season with salt and pepper.

3. Heat oil in a pot. Add onions and sauté briefly until translucent. Pour in the broth, add the meat and cook for 11/4 hours over low heat.

4. In the meantime, clean, wash and halve the green beans.

5. Wash, peel, and roughly dice the potatoes. Wash the savory, shake dry and pluck the leaves off.

6. Add the beans, potatoes, and savory to the saucepan after 55 minutes and cook with them.

7. Wash the parsley, shake dry, pluck the leaves off and chop finely. Peel the horseradish and grate finely.

8. Add the parsley to the stew, season with salt and pepper. Serve the horseradish separately with the stew.

Kale Quinoa With Salmon

Preparation: 40 min

Nutritional values:

- Calories: 379 kcal (18%)
- Protein: 28g (29%)
- Fat: 16g (14%)
- Carbohydrates: 27g (18%)
- Added sugar: 1g (4%)
- Fiber: 6.1g (20%)

Ingredients:

- 340ml Vegetable broth
- 150g Quinoa
- 500g Kale
- Iodized salt with fluoride
- 400g Salmon fillet
- 2 Tsp. Olive oil

- 40ml of Apple juice

- 1 Tbsp. Wine vinegar

- 1 Tbsp. Lemon juice

- 7g Mustard (1 Tsp.)

- Pepper

Preparation steps:

1. Bring 300ml vegetable stock to a boil in a saucepan. Rinse the quinoa with water, then cook in the boiling broth according to the package instructions for about 15 minutes until al dente.

2. In the meantime, clean the kale, cut out thick leaf veins, wash it, roughly chop and cook in boiling salted water for about 10 minutes. Then drain, rinse in cold water and drain well.

3. In the meantime, rinse the salmon fillet, pat dry, and season with salt. Heat 1 teaspoon of olive oil in a pan. Fry the salmon in it for 2–3 minutes over high heat. Pour in the apple juice and sauté the salmon for 8 minutes on low heat, turning once.

4. In the meantime, for the dressing, stir together the vinegar, lemon juice, remaining stock, oil, salt, pepper, and mustard. Cut salmon into pieces and mix with quinoa and kale. Spread the salad on plates and drizzle with the dressing.

Pasta and Asparagus Salad

Preparation: 20 minutes, ready in 35 minutes

Nutritional values:

- Calories: 306 kcal (15%)
- Protein: 16g (16%)
- Fat: 5g (4%)
- Carbohydrates: 48g (32%)
- Added sugar: 1g (4%)
- Fiber: 5g (17%)

Ingredients:

- 300g Green asparagus
- Salt
- 250g Whole grain pasta (e.g., spirelli)
- 10 Radish

- 1 Organic lemon

- 1 Chive

- 80g Smoked turkey breast (sliced)

- 1 Tbsp. Rapeseed oil

- 2 Tbsp. Sour cream

- Pepper

- 1 Pinch coconut blossom sugar

Preparation steps:

1. Wash the asparagus, peel the lower third, and cut off the woody ends. Cut the asparagus diagonally into 2 cm long pieces.

2. Cook the asparagus for 4-5 minutes in a large amount of boiling salted water and remove with a slotted spoon. Rinse under cold water briefly and then drain well.

3. According to the instructions on the package in boiling asparagus water, cook the pasta.

4. Meanwhile, the radishes are cleaned and washed, then cut them into thin slices. Use hot water to wash the lemon, rub it dry, and finely grate the peel. Halve that lemon and squeeze it.

5. Wash your chives, shake them dry, and then cut them into rolls. Cut the breast of the turkey into thin strips.

6. Drain and drain the pasta, collecting about 50ml of pasta water.

7. For the salad dressing, mix two tablespoons of lemon juice, pasta water, lemon zest, rapeseed oil, and sour cream in a large bowl—season with salt, pepper, and coconut blossom sugar.

8. Add asparagus, pasta, radishes, and chives and mix carefully—season to taste with salt, pepper, and the remaining lemon juice and serve.

Lentil and Kale Salad With Avocado

Preparation: 35 min

Nutritional values:

- Calories: 346 kcal (16%)

- Protein: 18g (18%)

- Fat: 9g (8%)

- Carbohydrates: 41g (27%)

- Added sugar: 1g (4%)

- Fiber: 10.6g (35%)

Ingredients:

- 250g Beluga lentils

- 400g Young kale

- 45g Walnut kernels (3 Tbsp.)

- 3 Tbsp. White balsamic vinegar

- 1 Tsp. Maple syrup

- 1 Tsp. Hot mustard

- Iodized salt with fluoride

- Pepper

- 3 Tbsp. olive oil

- 1 Red-peeled apple

- 1 Lemon (juice)

- 1 Avocado

Preparation steps:

1. Cook the lentils double the amount of boiling water for 20-25 minutes over medium heat. In the meantime, clean and wash the kale, pluck the leaves from the thick leaf veins, and cut them into small pieces. Roughly chop the walnuts. For the dressing, whisk the vinegar with maple syrup, mustard, salt, pepper, and oil. Mix the lentils with the dressing and let it steep for 5 minutes. Then mix in the kale.

2. Wash, quarter, and core the apple cut into narrow wedges and drizzle with half of the lemon juice. Halve the avocado, remove the stone, cut into thin slices and drizzle with the remaining lemon juice. Fold the avocado and apple wedges into the lentil and kale salad. Spread the salad on plates and serve sprinkled with walnuts.

Green Asparagus With Chicken Breast

Preparation: 15 minutes

Nutritional values:

- Calories: 365 kcal (17%)

- Protein: 37g (38%)

- Fat: 20g (17%)

- Carbohydrates: 8g (5%)

- Added sugar: 2g (8%)

- Fiber: 3.5g (12%)

Ingredients:

- 500g Green asparagus

- 1 Tbsp. Olive oil

- Salt

- 1 Pinch coconut blossom sugar

- 4 Eggs

- 2 Tbsp. Ajwar

- 120g Smoked chicken breast cold cuts

- Pepper

Preparation steps:

1. Wash and drain the asparagus. Peel the lower third of the sticks and cut off the ends.

2. Heat the olive oil in a large non-stick pan. Fry the asparagus stalks in it for about 10 minutes over medium heat, turning occasionally. Season with salt and coconut blossom sugar.

3. In the meantime, whisk the eggs with ajwar and salt in a small bowl.

4. Heat a small non-stick pan, add the egg mixture and let it sit over low heat for 3–5 minutes, occasionally pushing together with a spatula from the outside in.

5. Cut the chicken breast slices into strips about 1 cm wide. Season the fried asparagus with salt and pepper. Arrange with scrambled eggs and strips of chicken breast and serve.

Kale With Smoked Pork and Fried Potatoes

Preparation: 1 h

Nutritional values:

- Calories: 467 kcal (22%)

- Protein: 42g (43%)

- Fat: 16g (14%)

- Carbohydrates: 34g (23%)

- Added sugar: 3.4g (14%)

- Fiber: 10.5g (35%)

Ingredients:

- 150g Onions (3 onions)

- 20g Clarified butter

- 750g Kale (frozen, chopped, unseasoned)

- 200ml Classic vegetable broth

- 700g Kassler (boneless)

- 750g Small, waxy potatoes (e.g., triplets)

- 1 Tbsp. Rapeseed oil

- Salt

- Pepper

- 15g Raw cane sugar (1 Tbsp.)

- 15g Tender oat flakes (2 Tbsp.)

- Ground allspice

Preparation steps:

1. Peel and dice the onions. Heat the clarified butter in a large saucepan or roasting pan and steam the onion cubes in it until translucent. Add the kale and vegetable broth and bring to a boil.

2. Place Kassler on top and cook covered for about 40 minutes over medium heat.

3. In the meantime, wash the potatoes thoroughly, cover with water in a saucepan, cover and cook for 15–20 minutes.

4. Drain the potatoes, rinse in cold water, peel, and cool down a little.

5. Heat the rapeseed oil in a coated pan and roast the potatoes over medium heat for 5–10 minutes, moving the pan frequently or turning the potatoes. Add salt and pepper.

6. Sprinkle cane sugar over the potatoes and continue frying until they are golden brown and the sugar is liquid.

7. Take out Kassler and keep warm. Stir the oatmeal into the kale and bring to the boil—season to taste with salt, pepper, and allspice.

8. Slice pork and serve on top of the kale. Serve with the roasted potatoes.

Spinach and Celery Salad with Chicken

Preparation: 25 min. Ready in 35 min

Nutritional values:

- Calories: 323 kcal (15%)

- Protein: 32g (33%)

- Fat: 19g (16%)

- Carbohydrates: 4g (3%)

- Added sugar: 1g (4%)

- Fiber: 3.7g (12%)

Ingredients:

- 2 Chicken breast fillets approx. 140g each

- Salt

- Pepper from the mill

- 4 Tbsp. Grapeseed oil

- 40g Pine nuts

- 400g Spinach

- 2 Poles

- Celery

- 4 Spring onions

- 2 Tbsp. Vegetable broth

- 2 Tbsp. White balsamic vinegar

- 1 Tbsp. Lemon juice

- 1 pinch Sugar

- 40g Grated parmesan

Preparation steps:

1. Wash the chicken breasts, pat dry, season with salt, pepper, and fry for 2-3 minutes on each side until golden brown. Sweat the pine nuts with them, remove them from the fire.

2. Wash, clean, and chop spinach if necessary. Wash, clean, and piece the celery, wash, and clean spring onions and rings. Mix with broth, balsamic vinegar, lemon juice, and season with salt, pepper, and sugar.

3. Cut the chicken into slices and serve with pine nuts and remaining salad ingredients.

Chapter 4.   Casseroles and Pasta

Vegetarian Noodle Casserole

Preparation: 40 min. Ready in 1 h. 20 min.

Nutritional values:

- Calories: 644 kcal (31%)

- Protein: 33g (34%)

- Fat: 23g (20%)

- Carbohydrates: 73g (49%)

- Added sugar: 0g (0%)

- Fiber: 17.5g (58%)

Ingredients:

- 400g Whole wheat pasta, e.g., b. macaroni

- Salt

- 1 Pole leek

- 200g Broccoli

- 1 Red pepper

- 100g Dried tomatoes

- 4 Eggs

- 100ml milk (3.5% Fat)

- 100g Creme fraiche cheese

- 100g Grated cheese (e.g., Emmentaler, gouda)

- Pepper

- Nutmeg

Preparation steps:

1. In salted water, boil the macaroni until they are firm to bite, drain, and drain. The leek is washed and cleaned, then cut into rings. Set 1 handful of leek rings aside for garnishing. Wash the broccoli, separate the florets, dice the stem and peel it. Cook (blanch) together for 2-3 minutes in the salted water. Quench and drain it well. The peppers should be washed and cleaned, and cut into small pieces. Cut into strips with the tomatoes.

2. Mix the eggs with the milk, crème fraîche, and half of the cheese— season with salt, pepper, and nutmeg.

3. Mix the broccoli, leek, bell peppers, and tomatoes with the pasta and place in four single-serving oven dishes (or one large baking dish). Pour over the egg-milk, sprinkle with the rest of the cheese and bake in a preheated oven at 180 ° C (fan oven: 160 ° C; gas: level 2-3) until golden brown for about 30 minutes. Serve with the remaining leek sprinkled.

Lasagna With Spinach and Tomatoes

Preparation: 1 h. 30 min. Ready in 2 h.

Nutritional values:

- Calories: 626 kcal (30%)

- Protein: 25g (26%)

- Fat: 24g (21%)

- Carbohydrates: 76g (51%)

- Added sugar: 0g (0%)

- Fiber: 16.2g (54%)

Ingredients:

- 1 ½ kg Ripe tomatoes

- 1 Red onion

- 2 Garlic cloves

- 4 Tbsp. olive oil

- Salt

- Pepper

- Nutmeg

- 1 Handful basil

- 800g Fresh spinach

- 80g Butter

- 80g Wheat flour type 1050

- 1 l Milk (1.5% Fat:)

- 500g Whole grain lasagne sheets

Preparation steps:

1. Wash the tomatoes, scald them with boiling water, peel them, and cut them into small chunks. The onions are peeled and cut into fine pieces. Just peel the garlic. In a saucepan, heat two tablespoons of olive oil and gently sauté the onion. Add the tomato pieces and cloves of garlic and simmer on low heat for about 6 minutes, covered.

2. Remove the pot from the stove and season with salt, pepper, and nutmeg. Wash the basil leaves, shake to dry, and stir in. Cover and set aside.

3. Clean, wash and add the spinach in a large saucepan of boiling salted water over medium heat. Drain the spinach in a colander, place it on a cutting board, and chop finely. Pour into a bowl and season with salt and the remaining olive oil.

4. For the bechamel sauce, melt the butter over medium heat. Dust the flour over it and sweat it. Gradually, add the milk, stirring constantly, and bring to the boil, simmer on low heat for about 5 minutes while stirring, then remove the saucepan from the stove and season with salt, pepper, and plenty of nutmegs.

5. Put a layer of lasagne sheets in a baking dish. Spread a few tablespoons of tomato sauce, top with a little spinach, and pour a few bechamél sauce spoons over it. Now put on the pasta sheets

again and do the same again until all the ingredients are used up. Finish with the bechamel sauce.

6. Bake the lasagne in the preheated oven at 200 ° C (fan oven 180 ° C; gas: level 3) for about 30 minutes until a nice crust has formed. Cut into portions and serve hot.

Pasta and Cauliflower Casserole With Tofu

Preparation: 20 min. Ready in 50 min.

Nutritional values:

- Calories: 916 kcal (44%)

- Protein: 38g (39%)

- Fat: 47g (41%)

- Carbohydrates: 85g (57%)

- Added sugar: 0g (0%)

- Fiber: 13.8g (46%)

Ingredients:

- 1 Small cauliflower

- Salt

- 200g Smoked tofu

- 1 Tsp. Vegetable oil

- 400g Green ribbon noodles

- 1 Tomato

- 150g Grated vegan cheese

- Vegetable oil for the mold

- 50g Vegan margarine

- 2 Tbsp. flour

- 250ml of soy cream

- 120ml vegetable broth

- Pepper from the mill

- Freshly grated nutmeg

Preparation steps:

1. Wash the cauliflower and cut it into florets. For approximately 3 minutes, blanch in salted water. Pick it up, rinse it in cold water and drain it. Cut the tofu into small cubes and fry them until brown in hot oil. Remove and set aside afterward.

2. In boiling salted water, cook the pasta and drain 1-2 minutes before the cooking time is over, then rinse with cold water and drain. Wash the tomato, remove the stem, and cut it into slices. Grate your cheese coarsely.

3. Preheat the oven to an upper and lower heat of 200 ° C. Grease the baking pan. Heat the margarine in a saucepan, stir in the flour, fry until golden over low heat while stirring. Slowly, add the cream with the vegetable broth while stirring and bring to the boil, season with salt, pepper, and nutmeg. Spread the paste with the tofu and cauliflower florets in the baking dish and place the tomato slices on

top. Pour the sauce over it and sprinkle with the cheese; gratinate in the preheated oven for about 20 minutes.

Mediterranean Vegetable Lasagne

Preparation: 30 min. Ready in 1 h. 30 min.

Nutritional values:

- Calories: 452 kcal (22%)

- Protein: 21g (21%)

- Fat: 27g (23%)

- Carbohydrates: 31g (21%)

- Added sugar: 0g (0%)

- Fiber: 4.8g (16%)

Ingredients:

- 12 Sheets whole-grain lasagne sheets

- Salt

- 600g Ripe tomatoes

- 2 Small eggplant

- 2 Zucchini

- 1 Shallot

- 2 Garlic cloves

- 4 Stems basil

- 2 Stems oregano

- 2 Tbsp. Olive oil

- Pepper from the mill

- 1 Tbsp. Butter

- 1 Tbsp. wholemeal spelled flour

- 500ml milk (3.5% Fat:)

- Nutmeg

- 500g Ricotta

- 150g Grated gouda

Preparation steps:

1. Pre-cook lasagne sheets in boiling salted water until firm to bite. Remove with a sieve ladle and rinse well in cold water. Place them together on a kitchen towel. Wash your vegetables. Boil the tomatoes, rinse in cold water, peel, quarter, core, and cut into cubes. Clean and cut the eggplant into thin slices. Sprinkle the eggplant slices with some salt and let them steep for about 10 minutes. Peel and dice shallot and garlic. Wash herbs, shake to dry, pluck leaves from stems and chop finely. Dab eggplant slices.

2. In a pan, heat the oil and sauté shallot and garlic until translucent. Add the zucchini and eggplant slices on both sides until golden. Add the diced tomatoes and herbs, toss briefly, season with salt and pepper. Pull from the stove. Melt butter in a sauce for the bechamel sauce, dust with flour, let it take some color for a moment and deglaze with milk. Mix vigorously with a whisk to avoid lumps. Simmer and thicken over medium heat for 3–5 minutes, season with salt, pepper, and nutmeg to taste and remove from heat.

3. Line the bottom of an ovenproof dish with lasagne sheets if necessary. Mix the ricotta with the bechamel sauce, add salt, pepper, and nutmeg and distribute some of the lasagne base's mixtures. Top with some vegetables and another layer of lasagne sheets until all ingredients have been used. Finish with ricotta and sprinkle with cheese. Preheat the oven at 200°C (fan oven: 180°C; gas: level 3) for 40–50 minutes. Remove, let it rest briefly, and serve in pieces.

Pasta and Cabbage Casserole

Preparation: 15 minutes, ready in 45 minutes.

Nutritional values:

- Calories: 637 kcal (30%)

- Protein: 24g (24%)

- Fat: 23g (20%)

- Carbohydrates: 83g (55%)

- Added sugar: 0g (0%)

- Fiber: 19.1g (64%)

Ingredients:

- 500g Whole wheat pasta (farfalle)
- Salt
- 2 Carrots
- 500g Pointed cabbage (about 1/4 pointed cabbage)
- 2 Tbsp. butter
- 3 Tbsp. olive oil
- 150ml Vegetable broth
- Pepper
- 100g Grated mozzarella
- 2 Stems basil for garnish

Preparation steps:

1. Cook whole-wheat pasta in plenty of boiling salted water according to the package's instructions. Drain it.

2. In the meantime, peel the carrots and cut them into thin slices. Clean the pointed cabbage, cut into small pieces and wash in a colander.

3. Heat the butter and olive oil in a pan, fry the pointed cabbage and carrots in it. Deglaze with the broth, season with salt, pepper and cook over medium heat until the liquid has boiled away. Stir occasionally.

4. Mix the farfalle with the vegetables and spread it in a baking dish. Sprinkle cheese on top and grill in a preheated oven at 180 ° C (convection 160 ° C; gas: level 2–3) for 15–20 minutes. Garnish with basil.

Pasta and Potato Casserole With Onions

Preparation: 1 h

Nutritional values:

- Calories: 590 kcal (28%)

- Protein: 22g (22%)

- Fat: 31g (27%)

- Carbohydrates: 56g (37%)

- Added sugar: 0g (0%)

- Fiber: 4.1g (14%)

Ingredients:

- 600g Potatoes

- 300g Croissant noodle

- 2 Tbsp. Chopped parsley

- 50g Melted butter

- Salt

- Pepper

For pouring on:

- 400ml milk (replace 200ml with cream if you like)

- 4 Eggs

- 100g Emmentaler finely grated

- 2 Onions as desired

- 4 Tbsp. Clarified butter

- 50g Emmentaler

Preparation steps:

1. Peel the potatoes to cut them into bite-sized pieces, and cook in abundant salted water for 20 minutes. Following the package instructions, cook the noodles in abundant salted water.

2. Meanwhile, whisk the mixture together with the eggs. Season the milk with salt, pepper, and nutmeg, and add the cheese to the mixture. Pour half of it into a dish to bake. Drain the potatoes and pasta very well, mix in a bowl with the parsley and butter, pour into the baking dish, pour in the remaining egg, milk, and cover with aluminum foil. Cook at 200 °C for thirty minutes approx in the preheated oven.

3. Meanwhile, peel the onions, cut them into thin rings, and fry them until golden in the clarified butter. Out of the oven, take the finished casserole, cover, sprinkle with cheese and serve with onions garnished.

Vegetable Lasagna With Eggplant and Lentils

Preparation: 40 min. Ready in 1 h. 55 min.

Nutritional values:

- Calories: 486 kcal (23%)
- Protein: 23g (23%)
- Fat: 23g (20%)
- Carbohydrates: 47g (31%)
- Added sugar: 0g (0%)
- Fiber: 13g (43%)

Ingredients:

- 2 Eggplants
- Salt
- 1 Onion
- 1 Clove of garlic
- 2 Carrots

- 3 Tbsp. olive oil

- 1 Tbsp. tomato paste

- 150ml Vegetable broth

- 400g Chunky tomatoes

- 100g Red lentils

- 1 Tbsp. Butter

- 1 Tbsp. Wholemeal spelled flour

- 250ml Milk (3.5% Fat)

- Pepper

- 2 Tbsp. Freshly chopped herbs (e.g., rosemary and thyme)

- 6th Whole-grain lasagne sheets

- 150g Grated mozzarella

Preparation steps:

1. Wash and clean the eggplants and cut lengthways into slices about 1 cm thick. Salt them and let them steep in water for about 10 minutes.

2. Meanwhile, for the vegetable sauce, peel the onion and garlic, dice the onion and finely chop the garlic. Peel the carrots and dice them very small. Heat one tablespoon of oil in a large saucepan and sauté everything briefly over medium heat. Sauté tomato paste briefly, then deglaze with vegetable stock. Mix in the chunky tomatoes, add the lentils rinsed and drained. Simmer slightly thickly over low heat for about 10 minutes.

3. For the white sauce, melt the butter in a small hot saucepan. Stir in flour, sweat briefly, then pour in milk while stirring. Simmer over low heat for about 5 minutes until creamy. Remove from heat and season with salt and pepper.

4. Add the herbs to the vegetable sauce and season with salt and pepper.

5. Pat dry the eggplant slices. Heat one tablespoon of oil in a grill pan and fry eggplant slices in portions on both sides for about 2 minutes over medium heat until golden brown. Take out of the pan and place on a baking sheet.

6. Line a baking dish with a layer of eggplant slices. Spread about 2/3 of the vegetable sauce on top and cover with a pasta layer. Place the remaining eggplant slices on top and the rest of the vegetable sauce. Cover with pasta and brush with the white sauce. Sprinkle with the cheese and bake in a preheated oven at 180 ° C (convection 160 ° C; gas: level 2–3) for about 45 minutes until golden brown.

Chapter 5.   Chicken Recipes

Chocolate Chicken With Seasoned Rice

Preparation: 45 min. Ready in 1 h. 15 min.

Nutritional values:

- Calories: 722 kcal (34%)

- Protein: 50g (51%)

- Fat: 31g (27%)

- Carbohydrates: 57g (38%)

- Added sugar: 4g (16%)

- Fiber: 6.7g (22%)

Ingredients:

- 8 Ready-to-cook chicken pieces (approx. 1–1.2 kg; breast, wings, and thighs)

- Salt

- Pepper

- 70g Turkey ham

- 80g Shallots (8 small shallots)

- 3 Garlic cloves

- 2 Carrots

- 1 Pole celery

- 250g White mushrooms

- 2 Tbsp. Rapeseed oil

- 30g Wholemeal spelled flour (2 Tbsp.)

- 30g Tomato paste (2 Tbsp.)

- 100ml Dry red wine

- 2 Bay leaves

- 3 Stems oregano

- 5 Allspice grains

- 4 Cloves

- 3 Cinnamon sticks

- 500ml Chicken broth

- 200g Parboiled rice

- 50g Dark chocolate (at least 70% cocoa content)

Preparation steps:

1. Rinse the chicken pieces, pat dry, and season with salt and pepper. Chop the ham into small cubes. Clean or peel the shallots, garlic, carrots, and celery. Halve the shallots. Finely chop the garlic, dice the carrots and celery. Clean the mushrooms and leave whole or halve, depending on the size.

2. Heat the oil in a high pan. Fry the chicken pieces in portions for 5 minutes each over high heat until golden brown; then remove and set aside. Fry the carrots, celery, and shallots in it for about 5 minutes over medium heat. Add the mushrooms, ham, and garlic and fry for 3 minutes. Remove vegetables and set aside.

3. Put the chicken pieces back in the pan, dust with flour, stir in the tomato paste and let rhem caramelize for 2 minutes while stirring. Deglaze everything with red wine. Wash the bay leaves and two stalks of oregano, shake dry and add to the chicken. Add the spices except for one stick of cinnamon and two cloves, pour in the broth, and simmer for 30 minutes over low heat. Then add the vegetables again and cook for another 15 minutes. In the meantime, cook the rice with the rest of the cinnamon stick and cloves in 2.5 times the amount of salted water for 16-18 minutes.

4. When the meat is tender, remove the cinnamon sticks, bay leaves, and, if necessary, oregano, allspice, and cloves. Break the chocolate into pieces, mix with the sauce, and melt over low heat. Season the sauce to taste and garnish with the rest of the oregano. Serve the chicken with sauce and rice.

Lemon and Asparagus Chicken

Preparation: 20 min.

Nutritional values:

- Calories: 352 kcal (17%)

- Protein: 43g (44%)

- Fat: 12g (10%)

- Carbohydrates: 16g (11%)

- Added sugar: 0g (0%)

- Fiber: 5.2g (17%)

Ingredients:

- 1 Organic lemon

- 300g Chicken breast fillet (2 chicken breast fillets)

- Salt

- Pepper

- Paprika powder

- 30g Wholemeal flour (2 Tbsp.)

- 2 Tbsp. olive oil

- 500g Green asparagus

- 2 Garlic cloves

- 1 Tsp. mustard

- 100ml Vegetable broth

- ¼ Bunch fresh herbs (e.g., parsley or chervil)

Preparation steps:

1. With hot water, wash the lemon, pat dry, and cut it in half. Squeeze half of the juice out of the skin and rub it off. Cut half of the other piece into slices.

2. Rinse the chicken breast's fillets under cold water, pat them dry, and cut them in half horizontally. Season with the powdered salt, pepper, and paprika, and turn the flour over.

3. Heat 1 tablespoon of olive oil in a saucepan. On each side, fry the meat in it for 4–5 minutes over medium heat. Meanwhile, add the wedges with the lemon. Remove the lemon and the chicken, and set aside.

4. Wash the asparagus in the meantime, pat dry, and cut off the woody ends. Slice the asparagus into pieces that are about 4-5 cm long. Peel your garlic and chop it thinly.

5. Heat the rest of the oil in the same pan. Fry the garlic and asparagus pieces in it over medium heat for 3-4 minutes.

6. Add lemon juice, lemon zest, mustard, and broth, stir well, and briefly bring it to the boil. Reduce the heat, put the chicken breast fillet and lemon wedges back in the pan, and let them steep for a moment—season to taste with salt and pepper.

7. Wash herbs, shake dry, and roughly chop. Sprinkle over the lemon and asparagus chicken before serving.

Chicken Wrap With Peanut Coconut Sauce

Preparation: 20 min.

Nutritional values:

- Calories: 349 kcal (17%)

- Protein: 29g (30%)

- Fat: 20g (17%)

- Carbohydrates: 24g (16%)

- Added sugar: 2.8g (11%)

- Fiber: 6.7g (22%)

Ingredients:

- 2 Chicken breast fillets (150g each)

- 3 Tsp. Honey

- 3 Tbsp. soy sauce

- Salt

- Pepper

- ½ Cucumber

- 2 Carrots

- 4 Stems coriander

- 8 Sheets iceberg lettuce

- 100g Peanut butter

- 6 Tbsp. Coconut milk

- 1 Tbsp. Olive oil

- Cayenne pepper

- 4 Whole-grain tortilla cake

- 4 Tbsp. Sour cream

Preparation steps:

1. Wash the chicken breast, pat dry, and cut into strips. Mix 2 teaspoons of honey and one tablespoon of soy sauce in a bowl, season well with salt and pepper and marinate the chicken breast in it and let it steep for about 10 minutes.

2. In the meantime, wash the cucumber and carrot and cut both into fine sticks. Wash the coriander, shake dry and roughly chop the leaves. Wash the iceberg lettuce, pat dry and cut into thin strips.

3. For the peanut coconut sauce, put peanut butter and coconut milk in a saucepan and heat—season to taste with cayenne pepper, remaining soy sauce, and remaining honey.

4. Heat the oil in a non-stick pan, remove the chicken breast from the marinade and fry until golden brown on all sides over medium heat. Remove, set the chicken aside and wipe the pan.

5. Roast wraps in the pan without fat for about 30 seconds on each side. Then brush each wrap with one tablespoon of sour cream and top one half of the dough with chicken, cucumber, carrot, and lettuce. Drizzle with peanut and coconut sauce and sprinkle with coriander. Fold in the chicken wrap from below and roll-up.

Pancake Chicken Wraps With Lettuce and Sesame Seeds

Preparation: 1 h. 5 min. Ready in 1 h. 30 min.

Nutritional values:

- Calories: 464 kcal (22%)

- Protein: 44g (45%)

- Fat: 12g (10%)

- Carbohydrates: 42g (28%)

- Added sugar: 0g (0%)

- Fiber: 8.5g (28%)

Ingredients:

- 200g Whole-wheat flour

- 200ml Milk (1.5% Fat:)

- 200ml Mineral water

- Salt

- 3 Eggs

- 300g Chicken breast fillet (2 chicken breast fillets)

- 4 Tsp. Germ oil

- Pepper

- 200g Peas (frozen)

- ½ Lettuce

- 4 Stems basil

- 250g Low-Fat quark

- Paprika powder (hot pink)

- 1 Tbsp. Sesame

Preparation steps:

1. Mix the flour with milk, mineral water, ½ teaspoon salt, and one egg in a bowl to form a pancake batter. Cover and let it soak for 30 minutes.

2. In the meantime, rinse the chicken breast fillets, pat dry, and cut into long, narrow strips.

3. In a non-stick pan, heat one teaspoon of oil and fry the chicken strips for approximately 3 minutes over medium heat. Remove the salt and pepper from the heat.

4. In a small saucepan, bring a little salted water to a boil. Add the peas and cook for 2-3 minutes on low heat and drain. Rinse in cold water, allowing it to drain.

5. Fill the pot with water again and bring to a boil. Boil the remaining eggs in it for 8 minutes.

6. Divide the lettuce into leaves, wash, clean, and spin to dry. Rinse the eggs under cold water, peel them, and cut them into cubes with an egg cutter or knife.

7. Wash the basil, shake dry and pluck the leaves. Put some aside, cut the rest into strips and mix with low-Fat quark—season with salt, pepper, and paprika.

8. Stir the pancake batter. Dip a piece of kitchen paper in the remaining germ oil. Rub it into a coated pan (approx. 28 cm) and heat it.

9. Using a small spoon, pour 1/4 of the batter into the pan and distribute it evenly by turning it.

10. Sprinkle the pancakes with little sesame seeds and bake for about 2 minutes on each side—Bake 3 more pancakes from the rest of the batter and sesame seeds in the same way.

11. Let the pancakes cool a little on a plate. Then spread it out on the work surface with the sesame side down and brush with basil quark.

12. Place the peas and chopped egg in the middle of the pancakes, leaving an edge about 1 cm wide all around.

13. Pluck the lettuce leaves into pieces and distribute them with the pancakes' chicken strips. Fold the pancakes in the right and left so that the sides have straight edges.

14. Now roll up tightly from bottom to top and cut through the middle with a bread knife. Wrap the wraps tightly in paper napkins with the cut surface facing up and garnish with basil leaves.

Chicken Curry With Peppers and Zucchini

Preparation: 20 minutes, ready in 50 minutes.

Nutritional values:

- Calories: 397 kcal (19%)

- Protein: 44.5g (45%)

- Fat: 13.4g (12%)

- Carbohydrates: 23.8g (16%)

- Added sugar: 0g (0%)

- Fiber: 2.9g (10%)

Ingredients:

- 250g Brown rice

- 4 Chicken breast fillets approx. 150g each

- 1 Zucchini, small

- ½ Red pepper

- 3 Onions

- 2 Garlic cloves

- 1 Red chili pepper

- 3 Tbsp. Olive oil

- 1 Tbsp. Turmeric

- 1 Tsp. Chopped coriander root

- 1 Tsp. Freshly grated ginger

- ½ Ground cumin

- 350ml of poultry broth

- 200ml of coconut milk

- 2 Lime leaves

- Salt

- Pepper from the mill

- Coriander leaves or parsley leaves for the garnish

Preparation steps:

1. Cook or steam the rice according to the instructions on the packet.

2. Wash the chicken, pat dry, and cut into strips. Wash the zucchini, quarter lengthways, and cut into slices. Wash the bell pepper, cut in half, core, and cut into strips. Peel the onions and garlic, cut the onion into strips and finely chop the garlic. Wash and clean the chili pepper and cut into fine strips. Sauté with the garlic, zucchini, bell pepper, and onions in hot oil for 4–5 minutes while stirring. Add the chicken and cook for 2-3 minutes.

3. Mix in the turmeric, coriander root, ginger, and cumin and deglaze with the stock. Add the coconut milk and the lime leaves and simmer over low heat for about 15 minutes, stirring occasionally. If necessary, add a little more stock. Mix in the rice and finally season with salt and pepper. Garnish with coriander leaves and serve hot.

Chicken and Zucchini Salad With Nuts

Preparation: 30 min.

Nutritional values:

- Calories: 399 kcal (19%)

- Protein: 36g (37%)

- Fat: 26g (22%)

- Carbohydrates: 6g (4%)

- Added sugar: 0g (0%)

- Fiber: 4.1g (14%)

Ingredients:

- 3 Zucchini

- 500g Chicken breast fillet

- Salt

- Pepper

- 4 Tbsp. Olive oil

- ½ Fret mint

- ½ Lemon

- 80g Pecans

Preparation steps:

1. The zucchini should be washed and cleaned, and cut into thin slices. Rinse under cold water with the chicken fillet, pat dry, season with salt and pepper.

2. Heat the pan with two tablespoons of oil. Fry the chicken in it for approximately 10 minutes over medium heat until golden brown. Reduce the heat and let the chicken fillets cook.

3. In another pan, heat the remainder of the oil. Sauté the slices of zucchini over medium heat for approximately 4 minutes.

4. Wash the mint, shake the dried leaves, and pluck them. Squeeze half of the lemons together.

5. Take the chicken out of the bowl, drain it on kitchen paper and cut it into thin slices. Chop the pecans roughly and mix well with the zucchini, chicken, mint, and lemon juice. Use salt and pepper to season and arrange in bowls.

Chicken and Vegetable Skewers With Yogurt and Mint Dip

Preparation: 45 min. Ready in 5 h. 45 min.

Nutritional values:

- Calories: 215 kcal (10%)

- Protein: 33g (34%)

- Fat: 3g (3%)

- Carbohydrates: 11g (7%)

- Added sugar: 1g (4%)

- Fiber: 3g (10%)

Ingredients:

- 500g Large chicken breast fillet (2 large chicken breast fillets)

- 3 Onions

- 2 Rosemary branches

- 2 Thyme branches
- 1 Big lemon
- Salt
- Pepper from the mill
- 1 Tbsp. Olive oil
- 700ml Kefir
- 300g Yogurt (1.5% Fat:)
- 2 Tbsp. Cooking cream (15% Fat:)
- 1 Pinch of sugar
- 2 Tsp. Ground cumin
- 2 Fresh mint
- 1 Spring onions
- 250g Large yellow pepper (1 large yellow pepper)
- 16 Small cherry tomatoes

Preparation steps:

1. Rinse, pat dry, dice the chicken breast fillets, and place them in a bowl.

2. Peel the onions, dice them very finely and mix them with the poultry.

3. Wash the herbs and shake to dry. Strip off the rosemary needles and chop finely. Also, wipe off the thyme leaves. Halve and squeeze the lemon. Mix the rosemary, thyme, lemon juice, and oil into the poultry cubes—season with plenty of salt and pepper.

4. Pour the kefir over everything, mix well and cover with cling film. Let it steep (marinate) in the refrigerator for at least 5 hours, preferably overnight.

5. For the dip, stir the yogurt with the cooking cream, sugar, and cumin in a small bowl, then mix until they get smooth, season to taste with salt and pepper.

6. Wash the mint, shake dry, pluck off the leaves and put some of them aside. Cut the rest into fine strips. Stir into the yogurt mixture and let it steep in the refrigerator for about 1–2 hours.

7. Clean and wash the spring onions and cut them across into pieces about 2 cm long.

8. Halve, core, and wash the pepper and cut into 2 cm cubes. Wash and drain the cherry tomatoes.

9. Remove the chicken cubes from the marinade and allow to drain. Stick them alternately with peppers, spring onions, and tomatoes on long shashlik skewers.

10. Grill on all sides for 12-15 minutes on all sides, brushing with a little marinade several times in between. Garnish the yogurt dip with the remaining mint leaves and serve with the skewers.

Tomato Soup With Chicken Breast and Vegetables

Preparation: 15 minutes, ready in 30 minutes.

Nutritional values:

- Calories: 284 kcal (14%)

- Protein: 27g (28%)

- Fat: 8g (7%)

- Carbohydrates: 24g (16%)

- Added sugar: 1g (4%)

- Fiber: 8g (27%)

Ingredients:

- 400g Tomato puree

- 600ml Poultry broth

- 2 Carrots

- 200g Floury potatoes

- 2 Red peppers

- 200g Chickpeas (can; drained weight)

- 4 Spring onions

- 250g Chicken breast fillet

- Salt

- Chili powder

- 1 Lemon

- 1 Tsp. Honey

- 10g Parsley (0.5 bunch)

Preparation steps:

1. Bring tomatoes to the boil in a saucepan with broth. Meanwhile, peel the carrots and potatoes and chop them into small cubes. Halve,

core, wash and dice the peppers. Rinse and drain the chickpeas. Clean, wash, and cut the spring onions into rings. Rinse the chicken, pat dry, and cut into small cubes. Add everything together to the soup, season with salt and chili, and simmer over low heat for about 15 minutes, stirring occasionally.

2. In the meantime, squeeze the lemon and add about two tablespoons of juice to the soup along with honey. Wash parsley, shake dry, finely chop and sprinkle with the soup before serving.

Lentil and Chicken Salad With Arugula

Preparation: 1 h.

Nutritional values:

- Calories: 380 kcal (18%)

- Protein: 33g (34%)

- Fat: 17g (15%)

- Carbohydrates: 24g (16%)

- Added sugar: 0g (0%)

- Fiber: 10.3g (34%)

Ingredients:

- 300g Puy lentils
- 1 Red onion
- 1 Branch thyme
- 2 Tbsp. Rapeseed oil
- 1200ml of vegetable broth
- 1 Bay leaf
- Pepper
- 400g Chicken breast fillet
- Salt
- 500ml of poultry broth
- 250g Cherry tomatoes
- 80g Rocket (1 bunch)
- 3 Tbsp. Olive oil
- 2 Tbsp. Red wine vinegar

Preparation steps:

1. In a colander, rinse the lentils and drain them well. Peel the onions and finely chop them. Wash the thyme and dry with a shake.

2. In a saucepan, heat the rapeseed oil and sauté the onion in it until it is translucent over medium heat. Add the lentils and sauté for a short time, then pour in the broth. Add the bay leaf and thyme sprig, add the pepper and simmer for about 40 minutes over medium heat. Drain it then and let it cool.

3. Meanwhile, under cold water, rinse the chicken, pat it dry, season with salt and pepper. In a saucepan, heat the broth, put the chicken

in it, and let it simmer for approximately 20 minutes over low heat. Just take it out, let it cool down, and pluck it into pieces.

4. Wash the tomatoes in the meantime and cut them in half. Wash, clean, and dry the rocket with a spin.

5. Mix the olive oil and the vinegar for the vinaigrette and season with salt and pepper. On six plates, arrange the rocket, lentils, tomatoes, and chicken and drizzle with the vinaigrette.

Vietnamese Style Chicken Salad

Preparation: 40 min.

Nutritional values:

- Calories: 330 kcal (16%)

- Protein: 42g (43%)

- Fat: 13g (11%)

- Carbohydrates: 9g (6%)

- Added sugar: 0g (0%)

- Fiber: 5.2g (17%)

Ingredients:

- 700ml Poultry broth
- 600g Chicken breast fillet
- 300g Carrots (3 carrots)
- 200g Radishes (1 bunch)
- 1 Red chili pepper
- 1 lettuce
- Mixed herbs (e.g., mint, basil)
- 1 Lime
- 45g Chopped peanut kernel (3 Tbsp.)
- 2 Tbsp. vegetable oil
- Pepper

Preparation steps:

1. In a saucepan, bring the broth to a boil. Put the fillet of chicken breast in it and allow it to simmer for about 20 minutes over low heat.

2. Meanwhile, the carrots are peeled and cut into thin, long strips. The radishes are washed and cleaned, then cut into thin slices. Chili pepper is washed, cleaned, and finely chopped.

3. Wash the lettuce, dry it with a spin and cut it into fine strips. Wash the herbs, shake them dry, and pick the leaves off. Take the chicken breast fillet out of the broth, drain, and let it cool. Squeeze the lime.

4. Cut the meat into fine strips, mix with the prepared salad ingredients, lime juice, peanut, oil, and season with salt and pepper.

Chapter 6.   Launch and Dinner recipes

Thai Turkey Skewers With Onion and Peanut Sauce

Preparation: 50 min. Ready in 1 h. 50 min.

Nutritional values:

- Calories: 71 kcal (3%)

- Protein: 8g (8%)

- Fat: 3g (3%)

- Carbohydrates: 2g (1%)

- Added sugar: 1g (4%)

- Fiber: 0.5g (2%)

Ingredients:

- 500g Turkey escalope (4 turkey escalope)

- 1 Lime

- 1 Clove of garlic

- 3 Tbsp. Soy sauce

- 1 Tbsp. Dark sesame oil

- 4 Onions

- 125ml Classic vegetable broth

- 100g Peanut butter

- 1 Tbsp. Sugar

- Salt

- Chili flakes

Preparation steps:

1. Rinse turkey escalope, pat dry, and cut lengthways into five strips.

2. Pin each strip in a wave shape on one wooden skewer. Place the skewers in a large flat baking dish.

3. Halve and squeeze the lime. Put two tablespoons of juice in a bowl. Peel the garlic and squeeze into the lime juice through a garlic press.

4. Incorporate the soy sauce and the sesame oil. Brush the turkey skewers with it and leave for at least 1 hour to marinate in the refrigerator.

5. In the meantime, peel the onions and dice them. In a small saucepan, put the onion cubes and the broth and bring them to a boil. Cover and cook for approximately 20 minutes over low heat until the onions almost crumble, stirring occasionally.

6. Stir together the onion mixture with peanut butter and sugar. Season with salt, chili flakes, and 1-2 tablespoons of lime juice to taste. Dilute with a little vegetable stock if desired, and leave it to cool.

7. Drain the turkey skewers, place in a large aluminum dish, and grill on the hot grill for 8-10 minutes, turning several times and brushing with a little marinade. Serve with peanut sauce.

Green Asparagus Soup With Parmesan and Truffle Foam

Preparation: 40 min.

Nutritional values:

- Calories: 197 kcal (9%)

- Protein: 10g (10%)

- Fat: 14g (12%)

- Carbohydrates: 6g (4%)

- Added sugar: 0g (0%)

- Fiber: 2g (7%)

Ingredients:

- 250g Green asparagus

- 1 Shallot

- 10g Butter (1 Tbsp.)

- 400ml Classic vegetable broth

- 30g Parmesan (1 piece)

- ½ Lemon

- 4 Tbsp. Soy cream

- Salt

- Pepper

- 100ml Milk (1.5% Fat:)

- 3 Drops truffle oil

Preparation steps:

1. Wash and drain the asparagus and cut off any woody ends. Peel the asparagus in the lower third. Cut the sticks into pieces about 2 cm long. Peel and finely chop the shallot.

2. Heat the butter in a saucepan. Sauté the asparagus pieces and shallot in it over medium heat.

3. Pour in the vegetable broth and bring to a boil. Cook on low heat for about 15 minutes.

4. In the meantime, grate the parmesan cheese finely.

5. Add the parmesan to the asparagus and finely puree everything with a hand blender.

6. Squeeze the lemon. Stir the soy cream into the soup, season with salt, pepper, and a little lemon juice.

7. Heat the milk, a pinch of salt, and truffle oil (to approx. 60 ° C), do not let it boil! Whip the milk until frothy, e.g., with a hand blender, small whisk, or an electric milk frother. (The best results are achieved with low-fat long-life milk). Pour the soup into glasses or glass cups, distribute the milk foam on top. Serve immediately.

Marinated Scampi on a Tomato and Aubergine Gratin

Preparation: 30 min. Ready in 1 hour.

Nutritional values:

- Calories: 335 kcal (16%)

- Protein: 28g (29%)

- Fat: 18g (16%)

- Carbohydrates: 12g (8%)

- Added sugar: 0g (0%)

- Fiber: 5.5g (18%)

Ingredients:

- 6 Scampi (ready to cook; headless, with shell)

- 1 Chili pepper

- 2 Tbsp. olive oil

- 1 Clove of garlic

- 1 Onion

- 2 Thyme

- 1 Chive

- 200g Eggplant (1 eggplant)

- 300g Tomatoes (4 tomatoes)

- ½ Lemon

- 50ml Classic vegetable broth

- Salt

- Pepper

- 125g Mozzarella (9% Fat)

Preparation steps:

1. Cut the scampi's length on the back and remove the black intestinal threads. Rinse the scampi and pat dry with kitchen paper.

2. Halve the chili lengthways, remove the core, wash and finely chop.

3. Mix the chili and one tablespoon of oil in a small bowl. Put in the scampi and cover, and leave it to stand in the fridge (marinate).

4. Peel and finely chop garlic and onion.

5. Wash the thyme and chives and shake dry. Pluck the leaves from the thyme, cut the chives into rolls.

6. Clean and wash the eggplant and tomatoes and cut each into thin slices.

7. Layer the eggplant and tomatoes in a large flat baking dish.

8. Squeeze half of a lemon and mix the juice in a bowl with vegetable broth.

9. Stir in onion, garlic, thyme, half of the chives, and the rest of the olive oil.

10. Season well with salt and pepper. Pour the liquid over the tomatoes and eggplants and cook everything in the preheated oven at 180 ° C (fan oven: 160 ° C, gas: level 2–3) for 25 minutes.

11. In the meantime, drain the mozzarella, then cut it into slices. Spread the mozzarella on the vegetables. Bake for another 15 minutes and bake until golden brown (au gratin).

12. Before the cooking time, take the scampi out of the refrigerator. Heat a coated pan and fry the scampi with the chili oil for about 4 minutes. Sprinkle the rest of the chives on the gratin and serve with the scampi.

Chicken and Rice Pan With Broccoli and Corn

Preparation: 25 min.

Nutritional values:

- Calories: 352 kcal (17%)

- Protein: 27g (28%)

- Fat: 7g (6%)

- Carbohydrates: 45g (30%)

- Added sugar: 0g (0%)

- Fiber: 6g (20%)

Ingredients:

- 1 Small onion (40 g)

- 500g Broccoli

- 200g Corn (can; drained weight)

- 300g Chicken breast fillet

- 2 Tbsp. rapeseed oil

- 2 Packs of reis-fit express parboiled rice

- 3 Tbsp. lemon juice

- Iodized salt with fluoride

- Pepper

- Sweet paprika powder

- ½ Fret parsley (10g)

Preparation steps:

1. Peel and chop the onion. Clean and wash the broccoli and cut into small florets. Peel and cut the broccoli stalk. Rinse the corn kernels in a sieve and allow to drain. Rinse the chicken breast fillet, pat dry, and cut into small cubes.

2. Heat the rapeseed oil in a pan and fry the chicken cubes over medium heat for 5–6 minutes on all sides. Remove from pan and set aside. Then add the onion and sauté in the hot oil for 3 minutes. Add broccoli and sauté for another 5 minutes.

3. Loosen the rice by gently squeezing the packs, add rice with chicken cubes and corn to the broccoli, adding four tablespoons of water and lemon juice, and simmer for 2-3 minutes over medium heat.

4. Season the rice pan with salt, pepper, and paprika powder. Wash parsley, shake dry, and chop. Arrange the rice pan on plates and serve sprinkled with the parsley.

Pasta and Cheese Pan With Leek

Preparation: 25 min.

Nutrition Facts

- 388 calories;
- Protein 16.1g
- Carbohydrates 21.5g
- Fat 26.8g

Ingredients:

- 25g Walnut kernels (1 handful)

- 200g Whole wheat pasta (linguine)

- Salt

- 1 Pole leek

- 1 Onion

- 250g Chicken breast fillet

- 15g Butter (1 Tbsp.)

- 200g Cooking cream (15% Fat)

- Pepper

- 1 Tsp. Dried marjoram

- 100g Blue cheese (30% fat in dry matter)

Preparation steps:

1. Roughly chop walnuts and fry them in a hot pan without oil over medium heat for 3 minutes. Remove and set aside. Cook the pasta in plenty of salted water according to the packet's instructions until it is firm to the bite. Then drain it.

2. While the noodles are cooking, clean the leek, slit lengthways and wash thoroughly under running cold water, also between the leaves. Pat dry and cut everything into fine rings. Peel the onion and chop finely.

3. Wash the chicken breast, pat dry, and cut into strips. Heat the butter in a large pan. Add meat and fry over high heat for about 3 minutes. Add onion and sauté for 2 minutes over medium heat. Add the leek to the meat and cook covered for 2-3 minutes.

4. Pour in the cooking cream, mix in the pasta, and season everything with salt, pepper, and marjoram. Cut the cheese into small pieces, pour over the pasta and serve on plates with walnuts.

Rice With Chicken and Vegetables

Preparation: 50 min.

Nutrition Information

- Calories: 325,
- Carbohydrates: 34g,
- Protein: 13g,
- Fat: 15g,

Ingredients:

- 500g Chicken breast fillet

- 1 Onion

- 2 Garlic cloves

- 3 Spring onions

- 2 Red peppers

- 1 Pole celery

- 2 Chili peppers

- 3 Tbsp. olive oil

- 250g Natural long-grain rice

- 500ml Chicken broth

- 1 Bay leaf

- Salt

- Pepper

- 4 Tomatoes

- 4 Stems coriander

- ½ Tsp. Ground cumin

Preparation steps:

1. Rinse the chicken fillets under cold water, pat them dry, and cut them into strips. Peel and chop the onion and the garlic finely. The spring onions should be washed and cleaned, and cut into rings.

2. Wash the peppers, cut them in half, clean them, and cut them into strips. Wash and clean the celery and, with the celery greens, cut it into small pieces. Lengthwise, halve the chili, remove the core, wash, and chop.

3. In the pan, heat the oil. Over medium heat, steam the onion, garlic, and spring onions until they are translucent. Stir in the chicken and fry for about 1-2 minutes. Mix the paprika, celery, chili, and rice. Combine the bay leaf, salt, and pepper and pour in the broth. Cover and simmer for approximately 20 minutes over low heat, stirring occasionally.

4. Wash those tomatoes in the meantime. For peeling, use a kitchen knife to cut the tomatoes into a cross shape, scald them for a few seconds with boiling water, quench them and peel them. Cut the tomatoes into pieces and quarter them. Wash the cilantro, shake it dry, chop the leaves off. Mix in the tomatoes and the coriander when the rice is done. Use cumin, salt, and pepper to season.

5. Arrange the rice on four plates with the chicken and vegetables and serve immediately.

Italian Potato Salad

Preparation: 15 minutes ready in 1 h. 5 min.

Nutritional values:

- Calories: 295 kcal (14%)
- Protein: 6g (6%)
- Fat: 14g (12%)
- Carbohydrates: 34g (23%)
- Added sugar: 0g (0%)
- Fiber: 4g (13%)

Ingredients:

- 800g Small, fresh potatoes
- 1 Red pointed pepper
- 4 Tbsp. White balsamic vinegar
- 4 Tbsp. Olive oil
- Sea-salt

- Cayenne pepper

- 20g Parmesan 37% Fat

- 2 Stems of parsley

Preparation steps:

1. Wash the potatoes and cook them covered with salted water for about 20 minutes.

2. In the meantime, halve, core, wash and cut the pepper into strips. Mix the balsamic vinegar with the oil and season with salt and cayenne pepper.

3. Drain the potatoes, let them cool and cut into slices. Mix the potato slices, paprika, and dressing, season to taste, and let them steep for 30 minutes, stirring frequently. Meanwhile, grate the parmesan, wash the parsley, shake dry and finely chop.

4. Serve the cooled salad garnished with parmesan and parsley.

Potato Cucumber Salad

Preparation: 40 min.

Nutritional values:

- Calories: 270 kcal (13%)

- Protein: 12g (12%)

- Fat: 6g (5%)

- Carbohydrates: 40g (27%)

- Added sugar: 5g (20%)

- Fiber: 4.5g (15%)

Ingredients:

- 800g Waxy potatoes

- Salt

- 600g Stewed cucumber

- 2 Shallots

- 2 Tbsp. Rapeseed oil

- 350ml Vegetable broth

- 4 Tbsp. Fruit vinegar

- 2 Tsp. Raw cane sugar

- 2 Handfuls dill

- 150g North sea crabs

- Pepper from the mill

Preparation steps:

1. Cook the potatoes with water until they are tender. Drain and set aside.
2. Cut the cucumber with the peel into very thin slices (use the grater on the side of the slicer or the vegetable peeler) and add the salt.
3. Let it rest for about 20 minutes or until the cucumber dehydrates.
4. Place the cucumber in a colander to remove excess water and add the lemon juice.
5. Knead the potatoes, place them in an ovenproof dish, add the sliced cucumber with the lemon juice, the mayonnaise, the mustard and mix well.
6. If necessary, correct the salt. Garnish with lemon zest. Serve chilled.

Chicken and Spinach Pilaf With Yogurt

Preparation: 30 min.

Nutritional values

- Calories: 208 kcal
- Carbohydrates: 33 g
- Protein: 4 g
- Fat: 6 g

Ingredients:

- 300g Chicken breast fillet

- Salt

- Pepper

- 3 Tbsp. Peanut oil

- 2 Small onions (80 g)

- 300g Baby spinach

- 10g Herbs (2 handfuls; e.g., coriander, parsley)

- ½ Tsp. Ground cumin

- ½ Tsp. Ground coriander

- ½ Tsp. Turmeric powder

- 1 Tsp. Garam masala

- 500g Cooked basmati wholegrain rice (from the previous day)

- 50ml Vegetable broth

- 150g Yogurt (3.5% Fat:)

- Chili flakes

Preparation steps:

1. Rinse the chicken breast fillet, pat dry, and season with salt and pepper. Heat 1 tablespoon of oil in a pan. Fry the chicken fillet on both sides over medium heat for 5–8 minutes. Then take it out of the pan and let it cool down.

2. In the meantime, peel the onions and cut them into fine rings. Wash spinach, shake to dry and roughly chop. Wash the herbs, shake to dry, and also roughly chop. Cut the chicken into small pieces.

3. Heat the remaining oil in the pan. Sauté the onions in it over low heat for 5–6 minutes while stirring until golden. Stir in cumin, coriander, turmeric, and garam masala and fry for 1 minute. Add the chicken and rice and stir-fry for 5 minutes. Add the broth, the spinach and cook for 1–2 minutes. Stir the yogurt until smooth.

4. Season the pilaf with salt and pepper, distribute on plates and top with yogurt. Sprinkle everything with chopped herbs and chili flakes and serve.

Spinach Mashed Potatoes With Chickpeas

Preparation: 35 min.

Nutritional values per serving
- Calories: 439 kcal
- Carbohydrates: 117 g
- Protein: 34 g
- Fat: 30 g

Ingredients:

- 600g Potatoes

- Salt

- ½ Onion

- 150g Mushrooms

- 2 Tbsp. Olive oil

- Pepper

- 100g Baby spinach

- 200g Chickpeas (jar; drained weight)

- ½ Tsp. Cumin

- 230ml Oat drink (oat milk)

- 2 Tbsp. Vegan margarine

Preparation steps:

1. Peel and slice the potatoes into small pieces. In a saucepan, bring salted water to a boil and add the potatoes to it. Cook until the potatoes are cooked through, about 15 to 20 minutes.

2. Meanwhile, peel half of the onion, cut it into fine rings, and cut the rings in half again. Wash the mushrooms and slice them.

3. Heat the pan with one tablespoon of oil. Place the onion pieces in the hot pan and fry them for two minutes over high heat. Add the mushrooms to the pan and sauté. Decrease the heat and fry for 3 to 5 minutes until golden brown. Add salt and pepper to season.

4. In the meantime, in a colander, wash the spinach and drain, then set it aside.

5. Rinse the chickpeas under running water in a colander and leave them to drain. In a small pan, heat the remainder of the olive oil. Add the chickpeas and stir-fry over high heat for three minutes. Regularly swirl so that they do not burn. Remove from the heat and season with cumin and pepper.

6. Drain the potatoes, then bring them back to the pot. Add the oat drink, salt, and pepper, vegan margarine, and mash everything until you get a uniform puree. Add the baby spinach and mix until the spinach is incorporated into the pot. Arrange the mashed potatoes on two plates with the mushrooms and the chickpeas.

Asparagus With Egg Vinaigrette and Potatoes

Preparation: 1 h

Nutritional values:

- Calories: 313 kcal (15%)

- Protein: 17g (17%)

- Fat: 16g (14%)

- Carbohydrates: 23g (15%)

- Added sugar: 0g (0%)

- Fiber: 10g (33%)

Ingredients:

- 3 Eggs

- 1 kg White asparagus

- 1 kg Green asparagus

- Salt

- 1 Pinch coconut blossom sugar

- 500g Waxy potatoes

- 1 Radish

- 1 Chive

- 1 Box garden cress

- 4 tbsp. White wine vinegar

- Pepper

- 1 Tsp. Dijon mustard

- 4 Tbsp. Olive oil

Preparation steps:

1. Put the eggs in boiling water and boil for 8-10 minutes. Take out, rinse under cold water, and let them cool down.

2. While the eggs are cooking, wash the asparagus. Using a peeler, peel the white asparagus whole, only the lower third of the green. Cut off the woody ends roughly.

3. Put the peel and ends of the white asparagus in a large saucepan, cover well with water, season with ½ teaspoon salt and a pinch of coconut blossom sugar. Bring to the boil and cover, and cook over low heat for 20 minutes.

4. In the meantime, peel and wash the potatoes and cover with a little water and cook for 25–30 minutes.

5. Wash and clean the radish and cut it into fine sticks. Wash the chive, shake to dry, and cut into fine rolls. Cut the cress from the bed with kitchen scissors.

6. Pour the asparagus water through a sieve, collect the stock, return to the pot and bring to the boil again. Cook the white asparagus in it for 7 minutes, then add the greens and continue to cook for 4–5 minutes. The sticks should be done but still firm to the bite.

7. For the vinaigrette, mix the vinegar with salt, pepper, mustard, and 100ml of the asparagus stock with a whisk. Add oil and mix in.

8. Peel and roughly chop the eggs. Place the eggs, radishes, chives, and cress in a bowl. Pour over the vinaigrette and fold in—season to taste with salt and pepper.

9. Drain the potatoes. Take the asparagus out of the stock with a slotted spoon, drain briefly, and arrange plates. Spread the egg vinaigrette on top. Serve with the potatoes.

Asparagus Frisée Salad

Preparation: 45 min.

Nutritional values:

- Calories: 241 kcal (11%)

- Protein: 11g (11%)

- Fat: 15g (13%)

- Carbohydrates: 16g (11%)

- Added sugar: 1.3g (5%)

- Fiber: 6.3g (21%)

Ingredients:

- 750g White asparagus (or 500g ready-peeled)

- Salt

- 1 Tsp. Honey

- 30g Peeled pumpkin seeds (2 Tbsp.)

- 2 Slices of whole-grain bread

- 1 Shallot

- 1 Frisée salad (approx. 250 g, or dandelion)

- 4 Tbsp. White wine vinegar

- Pepper

- ½ Tsp. Mustard (medium hot)

- 3 Tbsp. Pumpkin seed oil

- 40g Thin slices of south tyrolean bacon (or bacon; 4 thin slices of south tyrolean bacon)

Preparation steps:

1. Wash the asparagus and carefully peel it with a peeler. Cut off the woody ends roughly. Bring salted water with honey to a boil in a large saucepan. Add the asparagus to the boiling water and cook for 10–13 minutes until al dente.

2. In the meantime, roughly chop the pumpkin seeds.

3. Cut the crust from the bread, dice the bread into small pieces. Peel and chop the shallot.

4. Clean the frisée, wash, spin to dry, and cut into bite-sized pieces.

5. Take four tablespoons of the asparagus stock and place them in a bowl. Add the vinegar, salt, pepper, mustard, and pumpkin seed oil—whip cream with a whisk. Stir in shallot cubes.

6. Heat a pan. Fry the bacon slices on both sides until very crispy.

7. Remove and drain on kitchen paper.

8. Put the bread cubes in the pan and fry them in the bacon fat until crispy.

9. Lift the asparagus out of the broth and drain. Arrange the frisée salad on plates, drizzle with the sauce, add the pumpkin seeds and bread cubes. Garnish with one slice of bacon each and serve.

Peach and Arugula Salad

Preparation: 30 min.

Nutritional values:

- Calories: 354 kcal (17%)

- Protein: 30g (31%)

- Fat: 19g (16%)

- Carbohydrates: 14g (9%)

- Added sugar: 1g (4%)

- Fiber: 4.5g (15%)

Ingredients:

- 120g Rocket (1.5 bunch)
- 4 Stems basil
- 3 Peaches
- 3 Spring onions
- 45g Pistachio nuts (3 Tbsp.)
- 450g Chicken breast fillet (skinless; 3 chicken breast fillets)
- Salt
- Pepper
- 5 Tbsp. Rapeseed oil
- 3 Tbsp. Red wine vinegar
- 1 Pinch sugar

Preparation steps:

1. Clean, wash and spin dry the rocket. Wash the basil, shake dry and pluck the leaves.

2. Wash peaches, rub dry, halve, remove stones and cut into 2 cm wide wedges.

3. Clean and wash the spring onions and cut diagonally into thin rings.

4. Roughly chop the pistachios and fry them in a small non-stick pan over medium heat without fat. Remove from the heat, place them on a small plate to let them cool down.

5. Rinse the chicken breast fillets, pat dry with kitchen paper, and cut into strips—season with salt and pepper.

6. In a large non-stick pan, heat two tablespoons of the oil, fry the chicken strips in it for about 5 minutes over high heat, and then remove them.

7. Mix the vinegar with three tablespoons of water, one pinch of sugar, salt, pepper, and the remaining oil in a large bowl to prepare the dressing.

8. Mix the peaches, the basil, and the spring onions in the rocket. Serve with strips of chicken and sprinkle with pistachios that have been roasted.

Cod and Pumpkin Soup With Potatoes

Preparation: 50 min.

Nutritional values per serving

- Calories: 236 kcal
- Carbohydrates: 47 g
- Protein: 3 g
- Fat: 3 g

Ingredients:

- 600g Hokkaido pumpkin (1 Hokkaido pumpkin)

- 700g Waxy potatoes

- 200g Leek (1 stick)

- 250g Fennel bulb (1 fennel bulb)

- Clove of garlic

- Tbsp. Olive oil

- 1 Tsp. Mustard seeds

- 500ml Classic vegetable broth

- 500g Cod fillet

- Salt

- 1 Organic lemon

- Pepper

- 1 pinch Ground cloves

Preparation steps:

1. Wash the pumpkin, cut in half, remove the seeds and the fibrous interior.

2. Cut the pumpkin meat into cubes about 2 cm.

3. Wash and peel the potatoes and cut into cubes about 2 cm in size.

4. Halve the leek lengthways, wash, clean, and cut across into 1 cm wide rings.

5. Wash and clean the fennel and put the greens aside. Halve and quarter the fennel and cut across into fine strips.

6. Peel the garlic and cut it into thin slices.

7. Heat oil in a pot. Add the pumpkin, potatoes, garlic, and mustard seeds and sauté briefly over medium heat.

8. Pour in the broth, bring to the boil and cook covered over medium heat for 8–10 minutes.

9. In the meantime, rinse the cod fillet, pat dry with kitchen paper, remove any bones and cut the fillet into strips about 2 cm wide.

10. Add the fennel and leek to the vegetables and bring to a boil.

11. Salt the fish, add it too and cover everything and cook for another 4 minutes over low heat.

12. Wash the lemon with hot water, rub dry and finely grate half of the peel. Halve the lemon and squeeze half (use the rest of the lemon later). Pluck the fennel into small twigs.

13. Season the fish soup with salt, pepper, garlic, and a little lemon juice to taste. Sprinkle with fennel greens and lemon zest and serve.

CONCLUSION

In the short term, the Lean & Green diet can help you to lose weight. However, as it can cause nutritional deficiencies as well as slow down the metabolism, it is not sustainable in the long term. Likewise, individuals whose illnesses require the consumption of specific foods, pregnant or lactating women, or medicated individuals should not be followed. Diets such as Mediterranean or Nordic are recommended in comparison to this dietary plan.